The Life of a Sculptor: Gozo Kawamura

The Life of a Sculptor: Gozo Kawamura

The Life of Gozo Kawamura: Japan's Forgotten Maestro of Sculpture

Nobuko Iinuma

Translation by Meher McArthur

Edited and Published by The Terasaki Nibei Foundation/
Naoko Anna Okada

Copyright © 2016 Nobuko Iinuma
All rights reserved.

ISBN-13: 9781539768180
ISBN-10: 153976818X
Library of Congress Control Number: 2016918048
CreateSpace Independent Publishing Platform
North Charleston, South Carolina

To Gozo Kawamura,
As a Japanese American, I offer this book to you with love.

Gozo working on the statue Authority of Law

Gozo making the prototype for the statue Authority of Law at the entrance to the US Supreme Court in Washington, DC, completed 1935 (U)

Foreword

Some Thoughts about the Unknown Sculptor Gozo Kawamura

By Masao Yamamoto, Director of the Shinano Art Museum, Nagano Prefecture

I am delighted that Nobuko Iinuma, a writer who literally lives between the United States and Japan, has written this biography of the sculptor Gozo Kawamura.

Despite his illustrious achievements, the name and work of Gozo Kawamura seem to have been forgotten, especially in Japan. This is particularly regrettable in our present global climate, when art is appreciated on an international level and cultural differences seem increasingly insignificant.

The artistic work of Gozo, who received his baptism in academism while studying the fundamentals of Western art in the United States and France, is perhaps a rare confirmation that this academism forms the very foundation of Western culture and always continues to exist as a deep source of creativity. Unfortunately, modern Japan has just started to learn the expression "Western academism," and because it has not yet grasped the greater, deeper aspects of this academism, our country has not been able to fully appreciate the extent to which artists like Rodin and the Impressionists were rejecting orthodoxy. In the space of one hundred years, many Japanese artists traveled to the United States and also to France to study. Because they faced various language barriers and other difficulties, the majority of them stayed abroad only long enough to enjoy a brief taste of the cultures they visited.

In Western society, since large-scale public sculptures are considered to be the ultimate expression of academic artistic production, the fact that much of Gozo's work is found in American public architectural works and sculptures suggests that he was exceptionally talented. But even though his skill was displayed in these monumental works, the fact that, in Japanese society, we still do not fully grasp the concepts of "public" and "common" works of art may be one of the reasons that, back in Japan, his achievements were not sufficiently appreciated and his name was lost in obscurity. This is why we should be thankful that the energetic and passionate efforts of Mrs. Iinuma, who is now an American citizen, have resulted in such a successful biography of Gozo.

Despite the fact that Gozo's talents were recognized in Europe and the United States and he worked hard on American public sculptures, his work on those sculptures was largely uncredited, and when he returned to Japan, he continued to be tossed around on the rough waves of wartime between Japan and the United States. In Japan today, his name must no longer be obscured. For this reason, the Shinano Art Museum is planning to hold an exhibition called "Kawamura, Gozo: 50 Years after His Death." Unfortunately, we will be able to exhibit only those sculptures that can be moved. His true talent can be seen shining from within his monumental sculptures elsewhere. I hope that this biography, which describes his great efforts, will convey to many people the breadth of his work.

As well as expressing my respect to Mrs. Iinuma for her tremendous efforts, I also wish to convey my hope that this biography will serve as a new bridge of artistic exchange between Japan, the United States, and the rest of the world.

December 1999

Masao Yamamoto, director, Shinano Art Museum, Nagano Prefecture

Contents

	Foreword · vii
One	**The Occupation Forces (Age Sixty-one)** · · · · · · · · · · · · · · 1
	General MacArthur Comes to Japan · · · · · · · · · · · · · · · · · 1
	Translating for the Occupation Forces · · · · · · · · · · · · · · · 3
	Gozo's Appointment as Principal Art Advisor for the US Forces in Yokosuka · 5
	Creating a Bust Sculpture of General MacArthur · · · · · · · 8
	The "Save Gozo!" Campaign · 10
Two	**Mountains and Rivers (Age Thirteen)** · · · · · · · · · · · · · · · · 13
	Gozo's Birthplace, Usuda Village in Shinshu · · · · · · · · · · 13
	Shinshu Ueda Middle School · 15
	Deciding to Become an Artist · 18
	Dreaming of Traveling to the United States · · · · · · · · · · 19
Three	**Journey to the United States (Age Twenty)** · · · · · · · · · · · 22
	Taking a Flying Leap · 22
	People Who Inspired Gozo to Travel Overseas · · · · · · · · 23
	Recording His First Steps in Boston · · · · · · · · · · · · · · · · 25
Four	**Studying in New York (Age Twenty-two)** · · · · · · · · · · · · · 31
	Entering the National Academy of Design · · · · · · · · · · · 31
	Feeling Destined to Be a Sculptor · · · · · · · · · · · · · · · · · · 33
	Considering Study in France · 36
Five	**Journey to France (Age Twenty-five)** · · · · · · · · · · · · · · · · 37
	Becoming MacMonnies's Assistant · · · · · · · · · · · · · · · · · 37
	Acceptance into the École des Beaux-Arts · · · · · · · · · · · 38

	Qualifying as the First Japanese Scholarship Student····41
	Meeting Rodin and the Invitation to Become
	His Assistant ····························43
	About His Mentor MacMonnies ···············46
Six	**Paris, City of Love (Age Twenty-six)** ·············**48**
	Pretty Girls·······························48
	Popularity with Girls·······················50
	The Joy of Youth···························53
Seven	**Return to New York (Age Twenty-nine)** ··········**58**
	The Challenge of Large-Scale Works ············58
	Completing *Civic Virtue*·····················62
	World War I ······························64
Eight	**Japanese Artists and Pioneers in the United States**
	(Early Twentieth Century)·················**68**
	Gozo's Notable Forerunners ··················68
	Japanese Artists Who Moved in Various Directions ·····70
	Japanese American Artists Who Were Sent to War
	Relocation Centers (Internment Camps)············74
Nine	**Marriage and Divorce (Age Thirty-two)**··········**77**
	Marrying Jeanie Farque ·····················77
	An Unhappy Married Life ····················79
	Gozo Creates His Masterpiece, *The Ideal Bull* ········83
Ten	**Shiori and Waka Yamada (Age Fifty-five)** ·········**87**
	Marrying His Better Half ····················87
	Shiori's Ability Blossoms·····················92
	Returning to Japan after Thirty-Six Years ·········96
Eleven	**Gozo's Friends (First Half of the Twentieth Century)**···**98**
	Toson Shimazaki, Hideyo Noguchi, and Others ·······98
	Establishment of the Gozo Kawamura Support
	Association ····························106
	Evacuation to Usuda, Shinshu ················108

Twelve	**Lois Johnson's Reminiscences (October 1998)**	**110**
	Finding a Living Witness	110
	An Excellent, Japan-Loving Apprentice	113
	The Enlarging Machine	117
	Memories of Gozo and the Cow	119
Thirteen	**People Associated with Gozo (October 1999)**	**121**
	Greater East Asia Group Sculpture Model Kazuo Hamada	121
	Masaji Watanabe, Gozo's Hospital Roommate	125
Fourteen	**Gozo Kawamura Materials**	**129**
	Gozo Kawamura Museum Pictures/Gozo's Home Pictures	129
	Gozo Kawamura Chronology	132
	List of Works by Gozo Kawamura	141
	Key to Photography Credits	144
	Reference Materials	145
	Acknowledgments	147
	Afterword	149

One

The Occupation Forces (Age Sixty-one)

General MacArthur Comes to Japan

On August 30, 1945, General Douglas MacArthur, supreme commander for the Allied powers, landed at Atsugi Naval Air Base in Kanagawa Prefecture.

The MacArthur who descended the landing ramp of his plane did not exude the fighting spirit of a war hero. Wearing sunglasses and clutching a corn pipe in his right hand, he stepped slowly onto Japanese soil. Around him, a military band sounded out heroically a line from the American national anthem: "'The star-spangled banner!" Right at the moment when the wind instruments reached a high pitch, General MacArthur faced the American soldiers with great dignity and saluted them.

Since the early dawn of December 7, 1941 (or in Japanese time, December 8), when the Japanese Imperial Navy had bombed Pearl Harbor on the Hawaiian island of Oahu, a horrific war had been raging in the Pacific for almost four years.

No one can erase from memory the horrors of life during the violent days of the war.

Depending on whether one was on the winning or losing side, emotions were entirely different. For the winners, memories of earlier suffering and sadness were mixed in with feelings of triumph and happiness as they raised their voices in victory. Those on the losing side, however, had lost their loved ones and seen the homes and possessions that they had spent years accumulating all turn to ashes. The futility and sense of total collapse formed a huge emotional wall over which the Japanese now had to try to climb.

On August 15, the Japanese people listened on radios full of static to the voice of the emperor announcing the end of the war. Even today, more than fifty years later, many Japanese clearly remember that strange day when, rather than wondering what would now become of them, they were thinking, "Ah, no more air raids, no more B-29 bombers."

Once the American soldiers began the Occupation, neighborhood associations told women to cut their hair short and stop wearing make-up. After September, however, even when the autumn winds began blowing through the burnt fields, the American soldiers showed no violence toward women or children.

One of the reasons for this was that Japanese authorities established the Recreation and Amusement Association (RAA), a system of prostitution and leisure facilities. The first of these facilities was in Omorikaigan in Tokyo's Ota Ward; soon, more were set up throughout the capital. Eventually, laws to eliminate of these prostitutes were established, but it took a considerable amount of time before police could completely enforce these laws. Until that time, because of the moral obligation to protect ordinary Japanese women, the Japanese authorities continued to conduct a profitable business with the American soldiers.

The ports were overflowing with vagrants and black-market activity. Not only in the big cities but all over the country, one could encounter the sight of young women wearing dark red lipstick, flapping their skirts around, and walking along hanging on to the arms of soldiers from the Occupation forces. All people could do was avert their eyes.

On the other hand, the novel sight of cars called "jeeps," with their fold-down roofs, driving smoothly over the bumpy roads was refreshing to the eyes of the defeated population, cheering them up enough to help them to forget their depression about having lost the war.

Children ran around after the Occupation forces, picking up the chocolates and chewing gum that the soldiers threw to them. They popped the gum into their mouths, gobbling it down because their stomachs were so empty.

The Americans set up their general headquarters (GHQ) in the Daiichi Seimei (Number One Life Insurance) Building in front of the Imperial Palace. They were charged with the task of managing and democratizing the population of a defeated, militarized country whose leader, the Emperor, was considered a god. From their headquarters, the American staff looked everywhere for solutions to this problem. The American policy of tightly guarding every single piece of information gathered by the Central Intelligence Agency (CIA) was absolute. However, General MacArthur recommended trying to understand the hearts of the Japanese people rather than trying to force a political revolution. Under his guidance, the Occupation forces worked with Japanese people in the cultural world, such as famous artists and sports figures, and provided them with encouragement and generous help. This collaboration by the Occupation forces extended as far as the administration of small towns in the countryside.

Translating for the Occupation Forces

One day, an order sent from a Major White, chief of the Occupation forces in Ueda City, Nagano Prefecture, was carried tightly in the hand of a prefectural-government-office employee to what was then the town of Usuda, in the Saku District in southern Nagano Prefecture, and into the hands of Gozo Kawamura.

To Mr. Gozo Kawamura,
You are being ordered to work as a translator
In the public relations office of the prefectural governor's office
January 30, 1946
Nagano Prefectural Government Office

Gozo Kawamura, while surprised to be summoned so suddenly from his life in rural Nagano, was at the same time pleased at the forthrightness of the American directive.

Just over five years before, in 1940, after thirty-six years living in the United States, Gozo had returned to his mother country, Japan. He had arrived at the port of Yokohama on November 10, 1940, a time when Japan still celebrated National Foundation Day, which commemorated 2,600 years of imperial rule with the Hinomaru flag and artillery salutes. He had never imagined that he would experience the bombing of Japan from the air by the United States, his second beloved homeland.

But in just those five years, the world had plunged into a state of unimaginable chaos, and Gozo was convinced that he would be killed. In the midst of war, he was scorned for being an American returnee and suspected of being an American spy because he spoke English, the language of the enemy country. Particularly during the two years when he had evacuated Tokyo and returned to his hometown of Usuda, Gozo and his entire family had been treated almost as outcasts. For Gozo, this period was so painful that he couldn't bring himself to take his sculpting tools out of storage and dust them off.

Now that Japan had lost the war, Gozo, who had been a young man of twenty when he had left Usuda thirty-six years ago with the hope of living a life of beauty and sculpture, was now white haired and bespectacled, living in a motherland that had been reduced to ashes. He had traded in his drafting pencils for a hoe, and he was now growing vegetables. So, when he received the command from GHQ, he immediately went for an interview with Lieutenant General Robert Eichelberger. Then he left Usuda, riding an American army jeep through Nagano Prefecture, and began his job as a translator, helping the Americans to close down Japanese military facilities and search for and confiscate weapons.

Gozo had mixed feelings about his new work.

His situation had turned around completely. Because he was now getting preferential treatment, receiving butter and sugar from the Occupation forces (the same soldiers who were strutting around Japan), he was getting cold looks from his own compatriots, who were gasping with starvation. Heavy-hearted, Gozo secretly hoped for the day that he could escape from this situation and focus entirely on the world of art again. Eventually, Gozo received orders from the Occupation forces to move from Usuda to Ueda City. He and his family then were transferred to Karuizawa.

At that time, the Karuizawa Prince Hotel had been requisitioned by the GHQ and was being used as a health resort, serving as a social venue for notable people from Japan and abroad. Being among the Americans there brought back memories that made Gozo feel rehabilitated, like himself again; he was no longer Gozo Kawamura, the translator, but was Gozo Kawamura, the sculptor. Americans had not forgotten that in New York Gozo had been a famous artist who made bronze sculptures and designed wall reliefs. He had received a second chance to enter the world of art.

The main figure responsible for Gozo's rehabilitation was Lieutenant General Eichelberger of the Eighth Division of the occupying US Army, who had respected Gozo and provided him assistance. Supreme Commander General MacArthur also helped in this, as did information the CIA gathered about him. Before returning to the United States, Eichelberger sent a concrete plan to help Gozo to the naval base at Yokosuka.

Gozo's Appointment as Principal Art Advisor for the US Forces in Yokosuka

In September 1947, Gozo moved from Karuizawa to Yokosuka and received the title of principal art advisor for the US forces at the Yokosuka base.

There, Naval General Benton W. Decker first provided Gozo with a studio. The space had originally been a Japanese naval officers' assembly room (the Enlisted Men's or EM Club), and it measured just under eleven thousand square feet. In this space, Gozo was free to do as he pleased. Once he got to Yokosuka, he went straight to work on his art.

In order to keep the Japanese under control and avoid bloodshed in occupied Japan, Supreme Commander General MacArthur had an ambitious Occupation policy that would involve reforming the imperial system without severing the bonds between the Emperor and the Japanese people. As a part of this policy, Decker made an attempt to promote Christianity among not only the American troops but also the Japanese citizens of Yokosuka. As part of this effort, they commissioned Gozo to create a statue of an angel for Easter.

The statue, which took Gozo two months to complete, was a two-meter-tall figure of an angel pointing toward heaven, to where Christ had ascended. On a label beside it was written, "He is not here but he has risen. New Testament Bible Luke Chapter 24, Verse 6."

On Easter Day, the citizens of Yokosuka mingled with the Occupation forces for the first time. To help them understand the meaning of Easter, on the first Sunday of April, they visited the exhibition venue and viewed the symbol of that day, Gozo's statue of the angel. Every year at Easter, this angel statue was brought out and displayed along the main road in front of the US naval base at Yokosuka.

From this moment, the relationship between Gozo and Naval General Decker was not that of victor and vanquished. Between them grew the warm, intimate relationship that forms between an artist and his patron. However, outside the blessed environment that Gozo was working in, the storm caused by the loss of the war had not abated, and the news was filled with reports of people starving to death in Tokyo and Osaka. At the end of the year, a large gathering was held at Hibiya Park to tackle the problem of the starving populace. Demobilized Japanese soldiers wearing army caps and military uniforms (of course without their rank badges) sold the people food and daily goods carried in on rain shutters. In no time, everything sold out. Things like cotton underwear and socks, which no one had seen during the war, appeared in abundance as if by magic. Just one year before, all of these items would have been rationed, but now they appeared with their clothing tags still attached. To Gozo, the strange scene made it seem that there had never really been a shortage.

While people were starving, Decker had made sure that Gozo had sugar, canned corned beef, and butter to eat. Gozo, who was embarrassed

The Life of a Sculptor: Gozo Kawamura

by this treatment, did his best to share all these foods with as many people he knew as possible. When he returned to Usuda to pick up some of the art tools that he had left in storage there, Gozo and his wife, Shiori, brought with them armfuls of food to give away. But the people of Usuda had found it hard to believe that Gozo had been a famous artist in the United States. Weighted down by their cold stares and their suspicions that, because he had come from the United States, he might be a spy, Gozo's back had become hunched over.

Watching Gozo quietly tilling the farmland that they had borrowed from his elder brother Kawamura Masutaro at the family home, his wife, Shiori, would always watch him and remember his sincerity and greatness as an artist in America. She wanted him to be able to stretch out his back and stand up straight again, full of the pride and confidence of someone who had built the giant four-meter-high alabaster statue *Justice*. Her sadness was almost as deep as Gozo's own.

However, those days had ended on August 15, 1945. Now, at last, many artists were coming again to Gozo's workshop in Yokosuka. Gozo was a small man, but because there always seemed to be a great warm glow around him, he had never appeared short, even among the tall Americans. Gozo and Shiori didn't imagine that they could easily return to the United States, but because they both understood Americans well, they secretly hoped a path would open to them.

On January 30, 1946, just five months after the war ended, it appeared that this hope would be realized, when the American Occupation forces had relaxed their policies a little and Gozo had received the orders from Nagano's prefectural government to work as a translator. The appointment was not for the Japanese translation department. Instead, the civil administration department of the American Information Bureau had put Gozo on the list of pro-American Japanese residents and had hired him to work for them.

Soon, Gozo was using his hands for drawing sketches again. First Lieutenant General Eichelberger and then Naval General Decker and his wife commissioned busts, but soon more and more commissions for work were coming to his studio on the American army base. In order to help Gozo earn a good living, Decker introduced many people to him. According to his records, the total number of commissions from just Americans was over thirty.

Creating a Bust Sculpture of General MacArthur

The people of Yokosuka were very grateful for General Decker's wise public-relations skills. As one expression of gratitude, the head of the Yokosuka Chamber of Commerce and Industry, Yoshinori Murata, commissioned Gozo to create a bust of General Decker, and he presented the statue along with a certificate of appreciation to General Decker on behalf of the citizens.

It was while he was working on the bust of General Decker that Gozo began complaining that he didn't feel well. Occasionally he had pains in his chest, and he felt continuous discomfort. But, because Naval General Decker was able to bring him some medicine from St. Luke's International Hospital, which the American troops were using, he was able to find some relief. Eventually, he completed the bust of Decker.

The work received praise from many people, and when he heard about the work, General MacArthur commissioned a bust of himself from Gozo. When they learned of General MacArthur's intention, various figures in Kanagawa Prefecture, such as Governor Yoshinaga Kato from the prefectural assembly, the mayor of Yokosuka, and a representative of the *Kanagawa Prefectural Newspaper*, all made their way to the American Embassy and requested to donate the statue to him. General MacArthur was extremely pleased with the statue, and later, when it inevitably came time for him to retire from his position as supreme commander, he took this statue, along with that of his son, Arthur, back to the United States with him. The statues were cast in bronze, and according to MacArthur, the statues of himself and his son were his most prized souvenirs from his time stationed in Japan.

The Life of a Sculptor: Gozo Kawamura

Later, early in the morning of June 25, 1950, war between South and North Korea broke out along the thirty-eighth parallel north, the border between the two countries. As North Korean troops advanced southward, the United Nations Security Council appointed General MacArthur the commanding officer of the UN forces, and on September 15, with the goal of helping the outnumbered South Korean forces, he landed with the UN forces at Incheon and eradicated the North Korean forces there. There, General MacArthur is said to have been planning to use an atomic bomb because it would give the UN forces a decisive victory against North Korea. However, it was clear that North Korea had the support of China and Russia. American President Truman, realizing that such action could trigger another world war, this time between the communist countries and free countries including Japan and Europe decided against MacArthur's diehard approach of ending the war in one destructive blast and recalled the general.

This incident came as a great shock to the Japanese people. They had become used to the toughness of General MacArthur, who had once been defeated by Japan and who had fled the Philippines and escaped to one of the US allies, Australia, with the famous words, "I shall return." Now, nine years later, on April 11, 1951, he declared, "Old soldiers never die; they just fade away," and quietly slipped into retirement. MacArthur returned to the United States with his wife, Jean, and their son, Arthur, and spent the rest of his days, months, and years in Connecticut peacefully, as if taking care of the various wounds he had received at the start of the war. In a field in South Norwalk, Connecticut, stands the headquarters of Remington Rand. Invited to become chairman of this firm, General MacArthur led a civilian life free from reports about military and foreign-affairs problems.

Dear Gozo
   The General and I both want to express our gratitude to you for the bronze bust of our little Arthur. Whoever sees it says it bears a wonderful

resemblance to Arthur, and I am certain that the statue was one of the General's most moving Christmas presents ever.
  We are praying for the happiness of your family.
  January 12, 1950
  Jean MacArthur

While the MacArthurs were stationed in Japan, Jean MacArthur wrote frequent letters to Gozo. For a military wife, who worried when her husband ran around brutal war zones, and who then in times of peace would help him rest, this consideration toward others was probably natural. She never forgot to send words of appreciation and gratitude to Gozo.

The "Save Gozo!" Campaign

The pains in Gozo's chest were not caused by heart disease, as he had thought, but by stomach cancer. The cancer that had appeared in 1959 had been treated for a while. But it eventually began spreading. While creating the bust of General MacArthur, Gozo realized that he was not going to live much longer. In his large studio, Gozo's gradually shrinking body would sink deep into his chair. Nevertheless, his bright spirit supported his slow-moving hands steadily as he passed the soldering iron across the surface of the statue.

While he was working on the bust of General MacArthur, a call to "Save Gozo!" started to rise up quietly from among the American soldiers.

Gozo had diagnosed himself with heart disease and neglected to get early treatment, and in the meantime, the cancer had spread so much that there was no way to treat it. Even the American military couldn't cure Gozo Kawamura. In 1950 there was no cure for cancer.

The Mainichi Shinbun of March 17, Showa 25 (1950) ran the headline "Save Gozo!" and printed a fully illustrated story of Gozo Kawamura's life and art with the following.

"Masterpieces Full of International Love"
"Old Kawamura of the Bulls"
"A Complicated Life"

The Life of a Sculptor: Gozo Kawamura

Five years before, American GHQ had ordered many of the staff among the American military forces stationed in Japan, including Lieutenant General Eichelberger, to search for Gozo Kawamura. General Decker, who had been attracted to Gozo's character, offered kindness and support to Gozo's family, even after Gozo's death.

In the end, Gozo was only able to complete the plaster prototype for the bust of General MacArthur. He passed away before he could finish the final bust.

His wife, Shiori, together with her daughter, Sachiko (Gozo's stepdaughter), hurried to complete the work. In order to make the bronze bust using the plaster prototype Gozo had created, they chopped firewood under the intense summer sun to fuel the foundry, and when they threw the wood into the flames, instead of giving them words of sympathy and praise, American soldiers from the base offered them help. Lieutenant General Birch, commander of the Far East Squadron, declared, "I would like to help complete the statue of General MacArthur!" He requested a donation of firewood for the foundry, and from Southeast Asia he obtained some suitable wood and arranged for it to be transported to the foundry.

That statue of General MacArthur was submitted to the third category (sculpture) of the 1950 (Showa 25) Nitten (Japan Fine Arts) Exhibition and won. In the October 29 issue of the *Mainichi Shinbun* newspaper appeared a quote from Shiori: "My husband is at peace" and a report entitled "General Ma: A collaborative work between Japan and the US." On November 28, an unveiling ceremony for the statue of General MacArthur was held at the Mitsukoshi Department Store.

Gozo was not able to return to the United States, but Americans returning home took many of his works with them. You could say that they found a peaceful home there again. Later, Shiori and Sachiko learned in a letter from Lieutenant General Eichelberger, who returned to the United States in August 1948, that the bust of General MacArthur had been installed in perpetuity as a memorial statue of the general at West Point. They surely conveyed this news to the spirit of Gozo.

Above left: Preparatory photograph taken by Gozo. Lieutenant General Eichelberger with black marks on his cheekbones, forehead, nose, and chin, applied by Gozo (left). (U)
Center left: Bust sculpture of Eichelberger completed in 1948. (Y)
Above right: Bust sculpture of General MacArthur, 1949 (Painted plaster. The bronze version of this sculpture can be seen in the General MacArthur Memorial Room at Daiichi Seimei Life Insurance Company in Tokyo.)
Below: Article about Gozo featured prominently in the *Mainichi Shinbun* newspaper. Afterward, the newspaper continued to report occasionally on his condition.

Two

Mountains and Rivers (Age Thirteen)

Gozo's Birthplace, Usuda Village in Shinshu

I rode the Koumi Line train from Komoro Station toward Kobuchizawa and passed through the rural district of South Saku. Looking through the train window, I saw the foot of Mount Asama spreading out before me. After going on a little farther, leaving Mount Asama behind, I passed through Nakagome Station and then Tatsuoka Castle Station. After traveling another forty minutes, I finally arrived at Usuda Station.

The station is very small, so small that it has no station employees. When I arrived there, I had to wait on the platform until my train departed before I could step off the platform, walk across the railroad tracks, and pass through the ticket gate. The one-story station building, when seen from outside, has the look of a shop. There are no gaudy advertisements on the walls. In the waiting room, all I saw were two passengers waiting for the next train. However, when I arrived there on May 9, 1997, my first time there, I didn't feel at all lonely. Rather, I had a sense of peacefulness; the stillness of the place was strangely reassuring to me.

I walked straight ahead out of the station, and in front of me flowed the Chikuma River. The Chikuma River flows northward, running parallel to the Koumi railway line. I took the bridge across the river and turned right, and as I walked along the embankment, I caught sight of the Saku General Hospital. Kawamura Gozo's house was number 173.

The station was built in 1915. This was the same year that the railway line was extended to the village of Usuda. This meant that when Gozo began attending middle school as a child in Ueda, the railway had not been built yet. Back then, the embankment of the Chikuma River was not as solid as it is today, so both the embankment road and the road through the town were probably dirt roads. Traveling from Usuda through Komoro and then on to Ueda must have taken almost a day. Because Gozo's eldest brother, Masutaro, and second brother, Seiichi, had already begun their time at Ueda Middle School, Gozo must have been excited at the thought of traveling with them to this unknown world.

In 1884, Gozo Kawamura was born the third son to his father, Kawamura Heijiro, and mother, Semu, who lived at house #173, Usuda Village, South Saku District, Nagano Prefecture.

For generations the Kawamura family had worked in the important position of magistrates for the Tanoguchi Clan. **Two storehouses containing family possessions were proof of the Kawamura family history.** These storehouses were quite splendid, according to Sue, the wife of Yojiro, a lineal descendant of the Kawamura family. Gozo later used the storehouses as his studio during the war, after he had returned from the United States and been evacuated to Usuda. Afterward they were dismantled, and now there is only an empty lot where they stood.

Gozo's maternal grandfather, Takeda Yoshidenji, was known for his talents as a writer, and he worked as private secretary for the Tanoguchi clan.

He excelled at poetry, especially haiku, writing under the pen name Ancient Cloud, and he lived life in the spotlight within the clan. He passed along this refinement and love of literature to his children and grandchildren. However, after Gozo's mother, Semu, had given birth to five children, she became very weak. Nobu, wife of Semu's eldest son, Masutaro, had to take care of Gozo and his siblings. Masutaro's eldest son, Sumio, and Gozo were only separated in age by three years, and every day they would play together outside until they were both covered in dirt.

The Life of a Sculptor: Gozo Kawamura

Shinshu Ueda Middle School

In 1891, Gozo entered Usuda Elementary School. Even though he was small, he was the leader of the neighborhood children. He was a very determined child, so he won the respect of his peers, but his sick mother worried from her hospital bed that she was to blame for his mischievous character because she was unable to discipline him properly.

When Gozo finished elementary school, he naturally followed in the footsteps of his older brothers and entered Ueda Middle School. However, the trip from Usuda to Ueda was twenty-five miles. At that time it was not possible to travel back and forth from Usuda to school in Ueda each day, so all seven children of the Kawamura family had to move to Ueda, where they lodged in a temple near Ueda Middle School. However, these mischievous children never seemed to be interested in studying. For them, moving from Usuda to Ueda was just like moving from the countryside to Tokyo today; to them, life in the bigger town seemed so exotic and exciting. In one of his letters home to his parents, Gozo wrote, "In Ueda, there's a festival every day." And Ueda Castle was much bigger than the ruins of Goryokaku, or "Five-Point Star Fortress," in Usuda, an important difference between the two towns in the mind of young Gozo.

To the east of Usuda in Tanomura, Lord Noritaka Matsudaira, chief of the Tatsuoka clan, who was descended both from same Matsudaira branch as Shogun Tokugawa Ieyasu and also from the Ogiyu-Matsudaira branch, was renowned from his youth as a wise and great man. In 1863, toward the end of the Tokugawa Shogunate's rule, he embarked on the construction of a five-point star fortress that resembled the design of French military engineer and architect Vauban. However, at that time, even though they were related to the Ogiyu branch, the shogun did not permit the Matsudaira family to have a castle on their domain; only encampments were permitted. Lord Matsudaira had started building his star-shaped castle, but because of these restrictions, it remained a small, flat, incomplete fortress, although it was still referred to as the "Goryokaku" or "Five-Point Star Fortress." It remained unfinished as the country transitioned into the Meiji period (1868–1912).

When Gozo was in elementary school, he and the other young boys from the village would often cross the Chikuma River, run all the way to the Goryokaku until they were breathless, and then lie on the embankment of the moat and gaze up at the sky. Later, on holidays and days when there was no school, he would go back there with his siblings and cousins. But now the freedom and brightness that they found in the town of Ueda appealed much more to the youngsters. And Gozo, carrying on his back his wrapping cloth full of underwear and food his mother had made him, made his way back to Ueda, and in this way the years gently passed by. Occasionally the mischievous young Gozo would receive letters from his concerned father telling him to do his chores at the temple and study hard.

Eventually, on March 30, 1903, Gozo graduated from Ueda Middle School with the hope of attending a university in Tokyo. However, around that time, one after the other, his parents passed away. This affected the lives of all his family members, especially his eldest brother, Masutaro. The family was resigned to the fact that their hospital-bound mother, Semu, would live a short life, but none of them had imagined that their father, Heijiro, would leave this world before she did.

At that time the rice shop that Heijiro had opened was flourishing. Whenever people went there to buy rice, he was somehow always able to accept whatever price they offered to pay him for it. His generous attitude influenced the local market for rice.

Masutaro took over his father's business and vowed with his younger brother Seiichi to preserve the Kawamura family. For the youngest, Gozo, who now fell under their care, this meant that the road to university was closed to him. Gozo was dazed; he now had no idea what to make of his life. Feeling a mixture of hope and confusion, he wanted to make money and help his family, but he couldn't figure out what he should do. What skills did he have that he could use to make money? He remembered his father telling him once when he came home from middle school in Ueda, "Don't worry about your mother. It's best to think about yourself and get an education. You don't know how long anyone is going to live. Don't worry about your finances."

The Life of a Sculptor: Gozo Kawamura

He wondered why his father, who had always been strong and healthy, would tell him something like that. Shortly after that conversation, when Gozo had gone back to school, a telegram had arrived saying, "Father suddenly ill. Come home." Gozo had jumped on board a train and ridden as far as Komoro Station, and instead of taking a horse-pulled carriage to Usuda, he ran all the way home. He ran those twelve or so miles as fast as he possibly could, as fast as any horse, and finally arrived home. By that time, his father was no longer able to recognize who Gozo was, but the young boy was glad to have made it home while his father was still breathing.

Above left: Graduation from Ueda Middle School, 1903 (Gozo at front right) (U)
Above right: Entering Ueda Middle School, 1897 (Gozo at right) (U)
Below: Ruins of the Goryokaku Castle, Usuda, Nagano Prefecture (National Historic Site) (U)

Deciding to Become an Artist

In the midst of his despair, Gozo suddenly realized what his skill was and what he wanted to do with his life. He wanted to be an artist.

He had always been good at calligraphy and building, and there was nothing he enjoyed more than drawing and painting. In both elementary school and middle school, he was always the best at drawing. But his relatives always warned him that he wouldn't be able to feed himself as an artist and that he should find another job with his hands. As his father had told him, he should get an education and go to college. But if he couldn't be a painter, then maybe he should study engineering…No, he should study art…He couldn't make up his mind.

Around that time, many of the young, strong kids in the village were talking about taking physical exams for conscription into the military. Gozo had never liked the idea of becoming a soldier, but the only way to get out of signing up was to go to university. So he decided to register for a course at a law college in Tokyo, as a way of avoiding conscription. He didn't particularly want to become a lawyer, and he couldn't travel to Tokyo, so he just hung around in Usuda. One day, he received an invitation from Mayor Akaoka Seikichi of Kirihara Village, where his elder brother's wife came from, to work as a substitute teacher at Kirihara Elementary School. If he took the teaching job, he would be able to postpone conscription, so Gozo happily accepted the offer. His monthly salary would be thirteen yen. It was certainly not a lot of money, but Gozo was thrilled that he didn't have to enlist in the army.

But six months after he began his job at Kirihara Elementary School, he received an expulsion notice due to his long-term absence from the law college in Tokyo, where he had never even set foot once. Because he had been using this fake student status as a way of dodging conscription, he received a notice from the Matsumoto Army Regiment that he would now have to take a physical exam for conscription. Gozo, who would do anything to avoid taking the exam, found himself thinking that he would one day like to travel overseas. He enrolled himself in an English language school, once again using the certificate of enrollment to appeal for a deferral of his conscription.

So, after less than a year teaching at the elementary school, he left the job and headed for Tokyo. His older brother Masutaro and his aunt, hoping that perhaps Gozo would be able to become a high-level government official, encouraged him, telling him not to worry about money for college. However, the young Gozo wrote in his journal at that time, "No matter how much money my brother and aunt pour into my career, there is no point. I wonder if in such a corrupt society as Japan is today, there are any scholars who actually want to become bureaucrats."

That year during the rainy season, the Chikuma River burst its banks and overflowed into all the fields along the riverside, causing a huge disaster. The damage affected the entire river basin, and from the Kawamura family to all the farmers of the Usuda Village area, the people of Usuda felt robbed of their strength and will to live. With this happening in his village, Gozo felt terrible that he was adding a further burden to his family by going to school.

Gozo, who had left for Tokyo, knew that even when he had finished his studies, he wouldn't want to go back to life in Shinshu or life in the countryside. However, even though as a child he had left Usuda and loved the newness and liveliness of Ueda, now that he was in the much larger city of Tokyo, he somehow didn't want to stay there.

Dreaming of Traveling to the United States

So, for the one-year anniversary of his father's death, he returned to Usuda and appealed to his two brothers for support. He declared to them that more than anything he wanted to become an artist and visit America to study. He was so passionate that he began to cry, and soon all three brothers broke down and cried together. So the three brothers went to their grandfather Kyuzo Kawamura. They told him together that Gozo wanted to travel to the United States, and begged for his permission. Although he was reluctant at first, Kyuzo soon gave his blessing, saying, "Well, if he wants to do this badly enough, he should do it!" Splitting the family into branches, his grandfather gave Gozo 2,000 yen, a sum he had calculated would be enough to cover his tuition in the United States for three years and provide a parting gift. His various other relatives also gave him parting gifts, and one of them, Hikoichi Miura (the grandfather in the main Miura family branch of the current mayor of Saku, Daisuke Miura) is also said to have sent Gozo financial assistance even after he had left for the United States.

By the exchange rate in 1900, one dollar equaled two yen. What seems like a small sum of money now was a fortune in those days. No one could predict when someone went abroad, when he would be able to return. It was possible that they would never see him again, so he even signed official documents stating that he had received his portion of the family estate.

Then, on July 25, 1904, Gozo finally left Usuda. On that day, a large crowd from the village joined his family to give him a warm send-off. Because saying good-bye was hard, the crowd ran after the horse and carriage Gozo was riding in for a long distance, but Gozo did not feel sad to be leaving his village. His father and mother were no longer living in the house he had grown up in, so he didn't really see it as his home anymore. Masutaro and his wife, Nobu, watched Gozo's back as he disappeared into the distance, and wondered about the place he was heading to. When Nobu in particular, who had loved and cared for Gozo as if he were her own child, thought of how much Gozo had wanted to leave Ueda after his parents died, she felt sad.

Nobu's father, Soemon Iijima, was the head of the village of Hiraga, and he enjoyed great popularity among his villagers. During the Mito Rebellion of 1864, just before the end of the Tokugawa period, the Tenguto army of Mito had arrived in Hiraga looking for lodging. The leader of the Tenguto, General Kounsai Takeda, who was also an elder of the Mito clan, was on his way to Mount Tsukuba to help his son Sakigake, who had raised an army there. Since Hiraga village was on the way, he asked to set up his headquarters in Hiraga for two nights.

Kounsai Takeda was a supporter of Nariaki Tokugawa, head of the Mito clan, and he admired Toko Foujita, who had promoted the Tempo

The Life of a Sculptor: Gozo Kawamura

Reforms, and had now become a staunch supporter of the "Revere the Emperor and Expel the Barbarians" faction that was gaining force against the shogunate. Placed in a predicament by Kounsai's sudden request, Iijima Soemon decided to let Kounsai's son Sakigake and Koshiro Foujita stay in his own house. The other four hundred men in the army were divided up among the other houses in the village and allowed to stay there.

This was a shock for the villagers of Hiraga. They were so poor that they barely had enough food for themselves. They weren't able to prepare meals and drinks. Furthermore, they were unable to do anything about the violent manner of the soldiers, who stole what precious food and money they did have, leaving the villagers with no means to live. To thank him for allowing them to stay there, Kounsai gave Soemon a spear and an iron fan, but Soemon always felt responsible for the Tenguto army's behavior, and since that time he had always felt bad toward the villagers.

Eventually, Japan transitioned into the Meiji Era, and when the privileges of magistrates and the sanctity given to old families were no longer protected, Soemon lost his position. He ended up stamping surety seals on other people's loans, essentially becoming their guarantor, and ultimately lost all his possessions. Nobu, Soemon's eldest daughter, who had witnessed this violent episode in minute detail, understood well the ups and downs of people's lives and fortunes. So, when she looked upon Gozo, it was with eyes full of care and compassion.

Gozo had felt Nobu's affection for him since he was a young boy, but his heart was already on its way to Yokohama. As his carriage headed toward Komoro Station, he watched the scenery that was so familiar to him recede into the distance. The Chikuma River, which had made Gozo seem heroic as he expertly swam in its strong current, and then the Katakai River both began to fade from view. Autumn had come early in Shinshu. The season for playing in the river had ended, and now it was time to play in the mountains. The mountains seemed to be beckoning him and his friends to go hunting for shiitake mushrooms, to race each other to find the mushrooms first. The mountains also faded behind him.

Three

Journey to the United States (Age Twenty)

Taking a Flying Leap

Gozo was scheduled to leave Yokohama on August 2, 1904, but his ship was delayed for a day. In February of that year, Japan and Russia had broken off diplomatic relations, and the Japanese navy attacked Russian warships stationed at Port Arthur, a Russian naval base on China's Liaodong Peninsula in the south of Manchuria. This began the Russo-Japanese War. The story of the Battle of Port Arthur was recounted by Lieutenant Hirose, Corporal Sugino Noboru, and others.

As newspapers printed news of this "courageous" war, Gozo repeatedly told his brothers that he hated war and couldn't understand why Japan had to engage in it. The soldiers were always the ones who died first. Soldiers were forced to enlist and were sent off to battle. The superior officers instructed them, "You've come here to fight for your country, so don't expect to go home!" When his friends in Usuda had enlisted, Gozo had told them, "Don't get killed. Make sure you come back home!"

Now Gozo, who was heading off to the United States, was feeling as nervous as any soldier going off to the battlefield. What were the

Americans like? From this moment on, Gozo was heading into a mysterious world that he knew little about.

People Who Inspired Gozo to Travel Overseas

The only person who Gozo had ever heard talk about life in foreign countries was Kiyoko Yamamoto in Yokohama. Her family was related to the Kawamura family and had a store. After the Meiji Restoration and the opening of Japan to the West, they soon began to trade with foreign countries. Their daughter Kiyoko was training to be a pianist and so had traveled to London and Vienna. Gozo found her various stories about the landscapes of Europe and the customs of British or German people fascinating, and soon a desire to go and see these places for himself grew within him.

There was another person who had influenced him: Banka Maruyama, a relative of Kiyoko's, so distantly related to Gozo. He had drawn Gozo into the world of art. Banka had traveled to the United States in 1899 and had held a solo exhibition of his watercolor paintings. Thanks to the Americans who were enamored by his paintings, he had been able to raise enough money to study in Europe. He had returned to Japan two years later and had shared with Gozo his countless observations of various different parts of Europe. He gave Gozo the names of two or three art schools in Britain and the United States, warning him that when at art school, he should first make sure to master the fundamentals.

A year after he returned to Japan, Banka had entered his work in the First Western Style Painting Exhibition and had received favorable reviews. So he left his hometown in Nagano Prefecture and his studio in Tsumura, moved to Tokyo, and set up a watercolor painting school in Misaki-cho in Kanda. While training the younger generation, he also entered his paintings *Moon over Burning Barley Fields* and *Summer Light* in the Meiji Industrial Exposition (held in Ueno Park, Tokyo, in 1907) to great acclaim. Seeing what Banka had achieved, when others told him that artists don't make enough money to eat, Gozo knew deep down inside that this wasn't necessarily true.

Many of Banka's landscape paintings depicted rural Nagano Prefecture. These elegant watercolor paintings rendered in gentle colors must have had a very different charm to the Westerners, who were used to seeing oil paintings. In particular, Americans seemed to deeply appreciate the refinement of Banka's paintings of the hydrangeas, rhododendrons, and camellias, flowers that Banka had become very fond of while he was living in the United States.

Banka had at first gained acclaim for his exhibitions of watercolor paintings and his pencil drawings, but after returning to Japan, he devoted himself to learning the Western-style painting of Hiroshi Yoshida, a master painter who served as one of the judges of the Japanese Art Academy (*Bunten*) exhibitions, and he became caught up in the world of Western painting techniques. The power of the Renaissance art that he had encountered while he was traveling in the United States and Europe gradually transformed Banka's painting style. Soon, Gozo was going to experience for himself, just as Banka had done, the world of this dynamic style.

Banka was supposedly the model for the character in Toson Shimazaki's novel *The Watercolor Painter* (*Suisaigaka*). Banka filed a complaint with the publisher, Chuokoronsha (from 1999 called Chuokoronshinsha), about this.

In the book, the watercolor artist Denkichi was based on Banka Maruyama, and the character Kiyono Yanagizawa was modeled after Gozo's relative Kiyoko Yamamoto.

After her studies abroad in Britain, Kiyoko had returned to Japan and become a pianist. In Shimazaki's novel, the characters Kiyono (Kiyoko) and Denkichi (Banka) were involved in an improper relationship. Because the daughter of one of the relatives of Banka's wife was also called Kiyono, this coincidence was a source of disharmony within the family, and it caused a lot of trouble for Banka.

Since this family drama was set in Shinshu, Banka found it hard to return to his hometown there. At that time, the author, Toson Shimazaki, was in love with a woman called Itoe Tachibana, and he frequently bumped into her in Karuizawa. Itoe lived with her mother in Shitaya in Ueno, and she was studying piano at Tokyo Music School. Toson met the beautiful Itoe somewhere and was so charmed by her that he too enrolled at the Tokyo Music School. Many of Toson's readers were aware of the connections between the character Kiyono and Itoe and between the watercolor painter Denkichi and Toson.

The publisher Chuokoronsha announced, "This controversy has disgraced our literary community." And they settled the case.

The ship that Gozo was due to leave the country on was delayed by one day, and it finally set sail on August 3. There was considerable panic on the ship when the passengers heard the news that two Russian naval ships were approaching Japan, but this news turned out to be a rumor. Staring at the islands of Japan as they gradually disappeared into the distance, Gozo felt no remorse for leaving his country. He could hear the sounds of many of the emigrants on the deck crying. He wondered where these people were moving to—probably Hawaii or the continental United States, but he didn't ask any of them. He felt that, although they all had different motivations for being on the ship, they were all (including himself) feeling a mixture of fear and hope. Among the people on board the ship, there were some who would succeed and return home loaded with honors, while others would disappear into misfortune in some corner of an unknown land. This twenty-year-old young man saw that he himself was feeling the same as each and every one of the other emigrants making this journey.

Recording His First Steps in Boston

When the ship docked in San Francisco, Gozo was so elated that he immediately forgot the seasickness that he had experienced for the whole two-week journey. He traveled alone to New York and visited with a friend of Banka's called Amano, who had already enrolled Gozo in an art school called Queen's Design School in Boston. Then, Amano took him to see his friend Bunkyo Matsuki, who acted as Gozo's guarantor. Gozo worked in Matsuki's shop during the day and in the evenings went to English and drawing classes. Although he had received enough money from his brother Masutaro, Gozo realized that, if he planned to live in the United States long term, he would need to earn some income too.

Bunkyo Matsuki had been born in April 1867 in Kamisuwa in Nagano Prefecture. When he was fifteen, he had entered a Nichiren Buddhist Seminary and become a priest, and as well as studying Chinese Buddhist texts, he had also studied English. However, his father's deep scholarly knowledge of antique calligraphy and painting had made a strong impression on him, and Matsuki longed to be in the world of art. He discarded his priest's robes and traveled to the United States, where he made his home in Boston. Through his connections with Professor Edward S. Morse, a great lover of Japanese culture, he eventually established himself as an art collector and dealer, introducing Japanese art to the United States.

In Europe it was Tadamasa Hayashi, but in the United States, Bunkyo Matsuki was known as *the* collector of Japanese art. When Gozo made up his mind to travel to the United States, after Banka Maruyama's introduction, Matsuki agreed to be Gozo's guarantor while he was staying in Boston.

Matsuki greatly appreciated the paintings of British artist James McNeill Whistler and promoted his work. In the beginning of the year 1900, he had helped Dr. Jokichi Takamine, a millionaire who was the only Japanese in American society circles, and his wife, Caroline, acquire one of Whistler's paintings. In Boston, Matsuki—who had been welcomed into the rich world of Japanese art by lovers of Japanese culture such as William S. Bigelow, Ernest F. Fenollosa (a professor at Tokyo University),

The Life of a Sculptor: Gozo Kawamura

and Tenshin Okakura—made many donations of art that can be found today in art museums and private collections.

It was very fortunate for Gozo Kawamura that he took his first steps into life in the United States in this environment.

In September, he visited the house of the American sculptor Henry Hudson Kitson (1863–1947) and asked him to hire him as a studio assistant. Kitson was a sculptor who happened to talk to Gozo at Queen's Design School when Gozo was drawing with a charcoal pencil for the first time. Gozo thought that having a close relationship with an American artist would be a great way to learn about art. Unfortunately, Kitson told him he wasn't able to take him on at the moment and suggested they talk again after Kitson had renovated his studio.

But Gozo didn't give up easily, and he visited Kitson's house again. Kitson wasn't home, so Gozo sat in the garden waiting in the strong August sun for Kitson to return. After a while, Gozo's stomach began to hurt from hunger. In the evening, Kitson's wife felt sorry for poor Gozo and took him to the party that her husband was attending. But again Kitson told him he couldn't hire him, explaining that his studio was small even for one person to work, and if he took on another person, there would be no room to move.

It might have been gastritis caused by nerves, but Gozo's stomach had been giving him trouble ever since he arrived in the United States. However, his single-mindedness—fighting back his stomachache and pleading desperately to do whatever Kitson needed, making plaster molds or anything—appealed to Kitson and his wife. They offered him the room above Kitson's studio. The wide room faced south. Kitson and his wife even put a bed and a dresser in it so that Gozo could live comfortably there. Gozo was so happy he could have taken flight.

Gozo now had his own place to live, and gradually he was becoming used to the English language, and so he was making more friends. In no time, the stomach pains that had been troubling him since he had arrived started to fade away.

Nobuko Iinuma

GOZO KAWAMURA 1904 IN NY

Banka Maruyama Post Cards (google)

Top: Commemorative photograph of Gozo in New York, 1904 (U)
Bottom: Exhibition catalog of Banka Maruyama (right) from Koumicho Takahara Museum in Saku, and one of his artwork of postcard (Views of Japan in Japanese Postcards)

The Life of a Sculptor: Gozo Kawamura

On November 3, 1905, eighty Japanese residents of Boston gathered together at the Brunswick Hotel to celebrate the Emperor's birthday. Gozo had heard that every year on the Meiji Emperor's birthday, Japanese people and Americans who loved Japan had been getting together and drinking champagne to celebrate, and that year he joined in. When the Japanese residents got together and started speaking to each other in Japanese, one American joined in their conversation. He had formerly been a teacher at a Japanese merchant marine school. When Gozo discovered that he had been teaching English in Japan at exactly the same time that Gozo had been studying English in Japan, he was so thrilled at the coincidence that he forgot to let go of his hand after shaking it. A number of Japanese exchange students and executives who had been in the United States longer than he had were engaged in a lively conversation about Yale and Harvard Universities' football games.

During that particular conversation, Gozo felt left out and lonely. His guarantor Matsuki consoled him by saying, "You are still young, so you don't need to play like that right now; you'll be able to enjoy yourself in due course." But to Gozo, these words didn't seem sympathetic, and at first he rejected them, preferring to wallow in self-pity. But then he pulled himself together and made a decision. He would not go to the theater, nor would he play cards. He vowed to stay away from billiards. Gozo could feel his natural competitive spirit rising up within him. And from then on, he kept a tight hold on that spirit.

In his sentimental moments, Gozo would gaze at the bay at the end of Fort Point Channel, and his thoughts would return to his hometown and the Chikuma River. Six months had already passed since he had left Usuda. And in that time he hadn't written a single line to his elder brothers or elder sister. In a journal entry at that time, he wrote, "Brothers and sister, please forgive me. If you are thinking of me, please try to understand."

His studies in Boston were much harder than he had imagined they would be. Gozo had not studied art while he was in Japan, and naturally it was hard for him to have to start studying from the basics.

At Kitson's studio, every day he built plaster molds for the busts, but no matter how much effort he put in and how much he concentrated on the work, he could not make a form that satisfied him. Gozo spent his days in a state of suffering and irritation.

Even though he knew this was his training, he still found the work frustrating. Perhaps Gozo's competitive nature was making him impatient, but feelings of frustration toward his teacher were welling up inside him. When he had spent a particularly difficult evening, he wrote in his journal, "If I tell people about my frustration, they will think I'm an idiot." Reading this, we can only wonder what he went through at that time.

He had really wanted to work as an artist's live-in assistant, but in the end he left Kitson's studio. He no longer needed to stay in Boston, so he decided to go to New York. Having made this decision, Gozo had an interview with R. T. Bain, a female professor in the Department of Sculpture in New York's National Academy of Design, and promised to work as her assistant.

Gozo's positivity was a good fit with the American character. Americans were people who genuinely recognized the results of hard work and the hard sell.

After Gozo had been in the United States for two years, he again began to feel lonely as he walked alone along the streets of New York City. On December 24, he stopped by Professor Bain's home and found Bain and her family right in the middle of a Christmas party. They were all opening presents calmly in front of the fire. They invited him to join them, but Gozo, as a foreigner, couldn't bring himself to spend even a moment in their happy family circle.

Resigned to being alone, he went outside and noticed that the moon was shining especially brightly that evening. As he stood alone gazing up at the moon, he felt a change taking place within his heart. He understood that here in New York, he was building the foundation for his future. He was small in stature, but even so, he felt a strange sense of dynamism rising up within him. He no longer felt envious of the Christmas tree with its colorful blinking lights or of the pile of presents underneath it.

This was the moment his life in New York finally began.

Four

Studying in New York (Age Twenty-two)

Entering the National Academy of Design

Gozo was living in Professor Bain's studio and working as an assistant as a requirement for studying at the National Academy of Design. First, he tackled the studio, taking just three days to tidy up the large, messy space and transform it into a studio that was easy to work in. In Bain's studio, there were a number of life-size plaster bust sculptures all arranged close together so that they were facing different directions. Gozo was so small that when people entered the studio, they couldn't find him unless they called out his name. While Gozo was reorganizing the studio, he somewhat strictly evaluated the skills of the other people working there. At that time, nine other assistants were working there. There were some who simply built plaster molds, and there were some technicians who were paid ten dollars per day, and other assistants who were paid one hundred dollars per day. At the time Gozo had assumed that all the artists working there were beginners, but he found out later that one of these men was a prominent American artist.

Eventually, when she saw the eagle finial for a flagpole for the US flag that Gozo had created for his first paid commission, Bain acknowledged Gozo's ability and hired him as an assistant operator of her enlarging machine.

This machine enabled sculptors to take small sculptures and enlarge them to create large-scale sculptures and reliefs. When he operated it, Gozo felt fired up inside. Every day, applying what little experience he had acquired by then to this new task and defying his physical exhaustion, he threw himself into the work. He didn't do it because the job was a means of earning money. Rather, he sensed somehow that this work was going to be useful to him in the future. Gozo was fascinated by the potential of this machine, and eventually he devoted himself to creating art using this production technique.

When he was not in Bain's studio, Gozo was studying art at the National Academy of Design, which had been established by Samuel Morse. In 1825 Morse, an electrical engineer, had invented the Morse code, a technology that had become the basis of modern communications technology in Japan too. The technology he developed to send the first telegram from Baltimore to Washington, DC in 1844 is considered along with radio broadcasting as one of the foundations of modern communication.

Morse also realized his goal of broadening the world of art by founding the National Academy of Design. In the early 1900s, when Gozo was enrolled as a student there, people who aspired to be artists longed to attend this "palace of art." Since Gozo's time, many other Japanese artists received their art training at this school and went on to create numerous works of art. As he learned the fundamentals of sculpture at the National Academy, Gozo's talent as an artist began to blossom.

With hard work, Gozo improved on the design of the enlarging machine and as a result succeeded in inventing his own original enlarging machine. Compared with the earlier machines, Gozo's was so much more precise and efficient that it won the complete confidence of Professor Bain. And the demonstration of such skill was a great asset for Gozo. Later, Mrs. Lois Johnson, who was Gozo's assistant and his lifelong friend, drew a diagram of the machine and explained that although the structure of the machine looked fairly simple at first glance, it was actually very difficult to operate. When Gozo was using it, he could make the enlargements very easily, but other people didn't have the same facility, and it seems that Gozo spent a fair amount of time carefully coaching others on how to operate it properly. Like a fish that had just found water, Gozo seemed reanimated by this invention, and he wore a happy expression that was very unlike the face he had worn in Boston.

Feeling Destined to Be a Sculptor

In the spring of 1908, Gozo had the sense that something important was about to happen. He wrote the following journal entry for April 3, a holiday to celebrate the Jimmu Tenno, Japan's first Emperor: "The fire in the fireplaces is still lovingly warm, and the garden is covered in white frost, but the songbirds and sparrows are starting to gather there. Spring seems just around the corner."

Gozo's heart was also looking for warmth. For some reason, he had a sense of longing, and his heart was somehow feeling full.

When he was living in Boston, he had become close to an older American girl. She had been generous to Gozo and had given the poor art student food and many other presents. Gozo had always accepted these gifts as tokens of her friendship, but one day, he received a passionate letter from her saying that she wanted to live under the same roof with him as his patron and support him for the rest of his life.

Gozo was so troubled by this that his stomach began to hurt. If he were to rely on her kindness, he would no doubt end up a third-rate painter. He shuddered at the thought. It now seemed that they couldn't continue their relationship as friends. He had come all the way to the United States so that he could become an artist, and it wasn't the right time for him to be getting involved with women. He couldn't let himself be weakened by love. He might be considered cold and ungrateful, but right now he had to get away from strong emotions. The need to flee from this difficult situation was probably one of the reasons Gozo decided to leave Boston and move to New York. He meant to leave his sweet and bitter emotions and memories behind in Boston and start a new life in New York, but he wasn't able to prevent the emptiness in his heart from gradually becoming larger.

On a few occasions, Gozo had considered himself popular with women. For sure, his cool eyes spoke of a sincere character, and the fact that he was only five feet two inches gave him a charm that seemed to trigger women's maternal instincts. Also, when he entered his studio wearing a white shirt and a scarf tied like a bow tie, he looked so stylish that he seemed more handsome than the taller men around him. However, because Gozo was still in the middle of his artistic training, he had to be careful in his speech and actions toward women. Even toward Professor Bain. He had to treat her as a professor, but because she was always very affectionate toward him, sometimes other people wondered if their relationship was more than that of professor and student.

No matter how good his English became, Gozo could never hope to have the mutual understanding that American friends had with one another. At times people thought he was a quibbler and stayed away from him, or conversely mistook him to be a simple man. To establish himself in a foreign country, there was nothing else for him to do but stop worrying about others and build up his own endurance and tolerance. In his life working as a studio assistant, he had to climb the stairs of progress one step at a time.

At one point when Gozo had just started work at the studio, Professor Bain's top apprentice, a Polish man called Hozinsky, left Gozo in charge of his work, took a break, and went back to his hometown of Buffalo. At first, Gozo was frustrated, thinking it was unfair that he had to keep doing his work and couldn't take time off, but then he went ahead and quickly completed Hozinsky's work, and his skill impressed Professor Bain. Then he realized that even though he was a newcomer, Bain and Hozinsky had deliberately chosen him from among her nine assistants and given him a special opportunity, and he had to respond to this trust by throwing himself into his work.

The Life of a Sculptor: Gozo Kawamura

Left: The National Academy, New York, 1999 (R)
Right: Above: At Conti's studio in New York, 1908 (Gozo at the left) (U)
Below: Gathering of artists before Gozo's departure to Paris, 1910 (Gozo in front row, third from the left) (U)

Considering Study in France

Five years had passed since he had come to the United States.

Gozo was approaching graduation from the National Academy when he first started thinking about traveling to France to study. It wasn't that the National Academy was lacking in anything; it was more that he had heard about France from his distant relative Banka Maruyama and wanted to go there and see it for himself. He wanted to visit Europe and see a Western culture that was completely different from his native Japan, one from which much of American culture had originated. Professor Bain gladly agreed to allow him to study abroad, and as a parting gift, she gave him a letter of introduction addressed to the American artist Frederick MacMonnies, who was residing in Paris. Later, this turned out to be the most wonderful of gifts. Whether our encounters with people will bring us great happiness or plunge us into the depths of despair, we can never know in advance. They are all controlled by the mysterious spinning wheel of fate.

Five years ago when he had set sail from Yokohama harbor, Gozo had stepped onto the ship full of uncertainty, his heart a mix of anxiety and hope as he started his voyage into the world of the unknown. But now, as he prepared to sail across the Atlantic to visit Europe, this young man was in a very different state of mind. His experiences in New York had taught him discipline and forced him to grow up. His training at the National Academy had provided Gozo with a foundation as an artist, filling him with an unwavering confidence and hopeful ambition.

Five

Journey to France (Age Twenty-five)

Becoming MacMonnies's Assistant

In the autumn of 1909, Gozo's friends waved good-bye as he set sail from the United States.

At that time, Gozo's knowledge of Europe consisted of the history he had learned at Ueda Middle School, to which he had added the overblown fantasies of his imagination. When he was in middle school in 1901, his history teacher, Mr. Fujisawa, shared his knowledge of the West with such a great passion that the students thought he must have been there himself. As he took notes with his brush, what had impressed Gozo the most was not the heroism of the Romans or their defeat of the European barbarians but the fact that the Romans had a sophisticated civilization long before the Japanese did.

For the time being, Gozo's destination was Paris. But he eventually wanted to travel to Italy and Greece. The sculpting and carving he had begun to study in New York was his foundation. Now, he completely immersed himself in learning how to create sculptures from drawings. Bain and Hozinsky had certainly recognized glimpses of Gozo's artistic talent in his works in New York. But at that time, no one, not even Gozo himself, would have predicted that Gozo would blossom in Paris, the City of Flowers.

When he arrived in France, Gozo immediately made his way to Giverny in the suburbs of Paris to meet the sculptor Frederick William MacMonnies.

Artists spend a lot of time absorbed in their art. They all seem to appear moody, not because they are rejecting others, but rather because they are not interested in anything or anyone who is not essential in the creation of the artworks that they are conceptualizing inside their own worlds.

MacMonnies was no exception. When Gozo visited him, MacMonnies seemed to have no interest in him at all at first. Before traveling to France, Gozo had wanted to find out more about MacMonnies by looking at his work, and his statue of a woman in the garden of the Metropolitan Museum particularly resonated with him. Gozo was deeply impressed by his work, and he asked MacMonnies several times if he would accept him as his assistant. Eventually MacMonnies agreed to take him on.

At first, Gozo visited the Louvre Museum every day. To him the collection of sculptures there was the best possible teacher, but just looking at them endlessly would get him nowhere. Knowing that unless he created his own works of art, he wouldn't bear any fruit himself, he bought some sketchbooks. In no time at all, he had filled them all up with sketches.

Acceptance into the École des Beaux-Arts

While living and working with MacMonnies, Gozo took the next step of preparing to take the entrance examination for the École des Beaux-Arts (now known as the École Nationale Supérieure des Beaux-Arts). At the time, many would-be artists from all around the world attended France's national art school, so the school exerted a strong influence on the world's artistic trends. Many young art students applied to the school, hoping to breathe in some of the creative spirit there, even just for a moment.

A few days before the examination, following the suggestion of a friend, Harry, who was visiting him in Paris, Gozo took his drawings to see if a Professor Eton would look at them. However, the professor wouldn't even agree to meet Gozo, let alone look at his drawings.

Gozo noted in his journal that this experience left him feeling emotionally unstable. He woke up at five in the morning, started worrying about the exam, and soon became overwhelmed by anxiety. Even after the exam was over, he couldn't calm his nerves for the rest of the day. MacMonnies joined Gozo in his unease, and the two spent many restless days together. In the time that Gozo had spent with him, MacMonnies had discovered Gozo's rare talents and had decided that he no longer wanted Gozo to merely be his assistant; he wanted them to work together as partners.

Despite all of this worry and the fact that entrance to the school was highly competitive, Gozo not only passed the entrance exam but did so with the second highest grade. He was so delighted to get into the École des Beaux-Arts, a school that he had admired for such a long time, that his heart danced with delight and continued to dance for a long time afterward. MacMonnies too was exceedingly pleased. In his journal for April 1912, Gozo wrote, "I am so happy! I want to remember this great feeling forever!" It had now been about two years since he had arrived in France.

Once he had been accepted, Gozo, who had now become familiar with life in Paris, vowed to distance himself from the world of smoking and drinking. In his journal he wrote the following:

Until about a year ago, I was able to drink a lot, but now I am a man of virtue, so I have to focus on my studies. Once you are familiar with the fleeting nature of life, the dust of hell is nothing special. You pass through the world of people, experience disaster and suffering, so you feel no pain. It is nothing to me now that I have endured great sadness and grief. Truly, for the first time since I left Japan for the United States, I feel like I have been able to breathe here. Passing the entrance exam in second place this spring was like a dream to me. I don't think it has made me conceited, but I certainly don't feel bad.

Top left: École des Beaux-Arts (Wikipedia)
Top right: Gozo as a student at the École des Beaux-Arts in Paris, always stylish (U)
Bottom: Bust of Gozo's teacher and mentor, MacMonnies. The work is unsigned, but an inscription on a photograph of it dates the statue to 1924. (Y)

Qualifying as the First Japanese Scholarship Student

One year later, Gozo took an examination to become a scholarship student and again passed it in second place—another dreamlike experience for him. Those students who ranked from first to seventh place were selected by the Sculpture and Drawing departments. As well as these subjects, they had to take exams in architecture, physiology, French language and world history. Gozo achieved almost perfect grades for these subjects too.

Now that he was a scholarship student, he was exempt from paying monthly tuition, and because he was being paid to work as MacMonnies's assistant, Gozo was feeling more secure than he had in a long time. At school, he was quite popular, and his time there was full of enjoyable episodes.

At that time, one of the students enrolled in the school was Egypt's Prince Mokhtar. Whenever it was time to sketch nude models, he would always take a seat in the front row and just sit staring at the model without making a single sketch. The models and other students couldn't stand him.

One day Gozo made a nude sculpture of Mokhtar and placed it right on the Champs Élysées. He painted the right half of the body gold and the left half silver. The statue drew considerable attention from people walking past. The police shrugged it off as just something art-school students do.

Clearly, Gozo enjoyed playing pranks. However, once when he heard that the other students were beating up the arrogant Mokhtar, he understood that this was an act of racism. Realizing that he too could be a target as an East Asian, he showed his noble side. By not joining the other students, Gozo weakened their efforts, and in the end the students abandoned their actions.

As would be expected from the top art school in the world, the lessons were taught at a very high level, and the teachers were very strict. In their basic anatomy class, students studied the human anatomy every week. More than just studying the human physique in detail, they had to use scalpels to cut into flesh precisely like a surgeon, slice by slice, and make notes about what they observed. Gozo's anatomical drawings have been preserved, and in them we see true beauty in the flow of the strands of muscles and meticulous detail in the surface texture of the bones. In work like this, we can see the evolution of Gozo's foundation, not as a painter, but as a man dedicated to sculpture. In his intense devotion to the art, Gozo knew that figuring out the internal structure of the body was fundamental to sculpture.

During the summer vacations, Gozo returned to MacMonnies's villa in Giverny, on the outskirts of Paris. In the summer, MacMonnies and his wife went traveling, and all his assistants took a break, so his studio was left empty. Gozo spent time reading books alone in the quiet of the countryside. Even though this time was very satisfying, he unexpectedly found himself feeling lonely and wishing he had a female companion.

While he was feeling lonely, the dog he had been keeping as a pet died of old age. Gozo had built a doghouse for him, but now he would no longer sleep there, so Gozo built him a grave by the tennis court. The death of his old dog, a companion who couldn't even speak, left Gozo feeling profoundly sad.

Some might laugh at the idea that Gozo was so sad at the death of his dog. But losing a loved one who had always been there, whether a person or an animal, can fill the heart with grief.

Some time before, MacMonnies had gone out, leaving some 10,000 francs in cash on the sculpting table in the studio. When he counted it, Gozo found 20,000 francs altogether. Mr. and Mrs. MacMonnies had always been very fond of Gozo, and they were both very generous with money. However, Gozo couldn't help but wonder whether MacMonnies had really simply forgotten the money in the studio or whether he was testing Gozo's honesty.

When MacMonnies came home and Gozo asked him, "Sir, why did you leave such a lot of money lying in a place like that?" MacMonnies rushed over to the studio to find it.

Laughing, Mrs. MacMonnies told him, "If you're looking for the money, Gozo put it safely in your desk drawer." With that, Gozo realized with a huge sense of relief that MacMonnies hadn't been testing him after all.

Meeting Rodin and the Invitation to Become His Assistant

During his time with MacMonnies, Gozo made many trips to the Louvre Museum. On one visit, he spent an entire day in the Michelangelo gallery, unable to leave. On another visit, he stood transfixed in front of a painting by Jean-François Millet, overflowing with admiration and sympathy. In the gallery of ancient Greek sculpture, he was overwhelmed by the figure of Venus, and in front of the works of Leonardo da Vinci, he was so moved that he almost stopped breathing.

Then one day this young Japanese man who was sketching enthusiastically in the galleries caught the eye of another visitor at the Louvre. It was Auguste Rodin. Rodin watched Gozo sketching from behind and began to wonder if he should ask this young man to work for him as his assistant. Eventually, having noticed each other at the Louvre on several occasions, they started talking. When Rodin discovered that Gozo didn't actually have a formal contract to work as MacMonnies's assistant, he asked if Gozo would be interested in working for him instead.

When Gozo told MacMonnies about this, the latter immediately replied, "Well, why don't the three of us meet and talk about this." He set up a meeting at a salon.

That day, Emile A. Bourdelle also unexpectedly attended their meeting. Bourdelle, who was born in the South of France, had entered the École des Beaux-Arts when he was just fifteen years old, and he was known there as a young genius. He was working in Rodin's studio and had gained Rodin's complete trust. Rodin always gave Bourdelle the most important tasks to complete, and in the art world he was known not as Rodin's assistant but as an artistic collaborator. Now that Rodin was becoming old, he was looking for an assistant for Bourdelle.

The four men—Rodin, Bourdelle, MacMonnies, and Gozo—engaged in a long, thoughtful conversation about their art and their work. Rodin, at the age of seventy, was a veteran and a giant in the art world. MacMonnies was about fifty and was an artist in the prime of his career, and Bourdelle was Rodin's main assistant. From Gozo's point of view, the three men were such giants that he didn't know what to say. It was just as if he was sitting an entrance examination. Nevertheless, he felt that all three of these men were keen to hear what he had to say for himself, so he little by little shared with them his observations and opinions.

In his late years, Rodin's style was going through an evolution from academic to grotesque. His statue of Balzac, which he himself believed to be a masterpiece, sparked one of the great art controversies of the nineteenth century, and it was so strongly criticized that Rodin left the work unfinished.

Rodin was transforming not only his sculptural style but also his techniques. Other sculptors created plaster casts of their clay models and then made copies from those. Rodin could create more realistic sculptures without the use of plaster casts. Since the Art Commission had recognized this technique in 1880, he continued to use it.

Rodin had been admired as France's leading artist. But now, more than twenty years later, perhaps because he was no longer fashionable, he was experiencing harder times.

Gozo was somewhat aware of Rodin's situation, so rather than discuss artistic theory, he decided to carefully study this man who might become his future teacher.

At the meeting, Rodin and Bourdelle offered to pay Gozo the highest salary, but since this was just their first interview, Gozo refrained from giving a definite answer. When he and MacMonnies parted company with Rodin and Bourdelle, MacMonnies asked him quietly, "Gozo, would you work with me even though I don't have much money?"

These words determined Gozo's course of action.

After that, Rodin asked Gozo two more times to work for him, but Gozo politely declined his invitation both times.

The Life of a Sculptor: Gozo Kawamura

There are some who would argue that Gozo turned Rodin down because their theories about art weren't compatible. However, when Gozo considered the fact that this man who was such an artistic giant had failed three times to get into the world's strictest art school, the École des Beaux-Arts, perhaps he thought that Rodin had been lacking something as a young art student. It wasn't that Gozo thought he was better than Rodin because he had been accepted into the school on his first try, but he did have doubts about the seriousness of Rodin's attitude toward art.

What was it about Gozo that had caught Rodin's eye? Once when Rodin visited Bourdelle, he saw his assistant wearing a Japanese summer kimono, or yukata, and was fascinated by the soft curves of the garment.

`On one of Bourdelle's shelves stood a Japanese Daruma doll. Rodin went up to it and picked it up. As he studied this doll with its bright red robes and huge round eyes, what could he have been thinking? When he was commissioned to create the statue of Balzac, he often thought of having Balzac wear the red robes of Daruma. The Red-Robed Balzac that he planned to make as a bust turned out in the end to be a figure of Balzac as Red-Robed Daruma. Rodin's interest in Japan was certainly first sparked by Bourdelle's yukata, a sort of Buddhist monk's robe. In 1980, Rodin's sculpture called *Figure of Hanako* was discovered in the depths of the Musée Guimet in France, where it had been hidden for a long time. So, Rodin was interested in Japanese people. We do not know when this work was made, but Bourdelle may have given it the name *Hanako*.

When Rodin saw the young Japanese artist sketching at the Louvre, of course he was impressed by Gozo's skill, but he also had a fascination for East Asian people.

Because the great Rodin had stopped to watch him sketch, Gozo became the envy of many other sculptors. Some of them suggested that Gozo must have had a dispute with Rodin and alienated him, since it was impossible that he could have turned down the chance to work as his assistant. Gozo was certainly ambitious and confident, but he wasn't that conceited. From his experiences in Boston and New York, Gozo well knew how hard it was to survive in this world. It was impossible to count the tears he had shed because he yearned for love, because he missed his home, because his work was hard. Every night, he lay alone on his bed looking up at the ceiling, and tears moistened his pillow.

About His Mentor MacMonnies

There was no way for Gozo to know whether his decision to choose MacMonnies as his teacher would lead to success or regret.

MacMonnies didn't have much money, but he had left Paris and built in Giverny a magnificent mansion with a huge garden that was more like a park. In 1883, Claude Monet had moved from Paris to Giverny and painted roads lined with poplar trees. MacMonnies's garden had areas that looked just like these paintings. Gozo was able to freely use the atelier in the mansion and the studio in the garden for his work.

Mrs. MacMonnies was a highly talented American woman who had graduated with honors from the National Academy.

Frederick William MacMonnies was born in 1863 in Brooklyn, New York. At the age of twenty-one, he moved to France. After entering the École des Beaux-Arts, he worked as an assistant to Augustus Saint-Gaudens.

Saint-Gaudens had emigrated from Ireland to the United States with both of his parents, and when he was thirteen, he started working with his father cutting cameos. Noticing his son's artistic talent, his father sent him to study at the National Academy of Design. In 1867, at the age of seventeen, at his father's suggestion, he went to Paris and enrolled at the École des Beaux-Arts and studied sculpture under Francois Jouffroy.

On his travels to Italy, at the San Giovanni Baptistery in Florence, Saint-Gaudens was exceedingly inspired by the great Renaissance sculptor Lorenzo Ghiberti's (1378–1455) bronze doors known as the *Gates of Paradise*. On each of the bronze panels, tales from the Old Testament Bible were depicted meticulously with precision and strength.

Saint-Gaudens was also heavily influenced by Donatello's wooden figure of Mary Magdalene, known as the *Penitent Magdalene*, which he saw at the Duomo Museum (Museum dell'Opera del Duomo) in Florence.

Saint-Gaudens's most representative work is a gilt-bronze statue of a heroic General William Sherman that towers over Central Park in New York City (at the intersection of Fifty-Seventh Street and Fifth Avenue). This statue is a memorial to one of the great men of the American Civil War. Sherman is shown advancing bravely on horseback, accompanied by a winged goddess. This statue is a work from Saint-Gaudens's most illustrious period. In this way, Saint-Gaudens, who had great admiration for Italian Renaissance sculpture, brought back to the United States what he'd learned while in France.

However, MacMonnies, who had apprenticed to Saint-Gaudens for five years, stayed behind in France when his teacher returned to the United States and devoted himself to his work. Some of MacMonnies's work can be seen at the Metropolitan Museum of Art in New York and at the Boston City Library courtyard. His masterpiece, a statue of Columbia (the female personification of the United States), commissioned for the 1893 World's Columbian Exposition in Chicago, won him the greatest acclaim.

Working with MacMonnies, Gozo was able not only to absorb through his teacher some of the artistic style of Saint-Gaudens, but also to draw upon some of the energy of the other young artists in MacMonnies's circle and use this to nourish his own creativity.

Mr. and Mrs. MacMonnies didn't have any children. They showed Gozo so much love that it was almost as if they had adopted him as their son. MacMonnies didn't treat Gozo simply as his assistant, and he gave him plenty of free time to work on his own art.

Six

Paris, City of Love (Age Twenty-six)

Pretty Girls

Love can suddenly appear right in front of you, and it can disappear just as quickly. This is how Gozo always looked at this emotion. However, he was never hurt by love. In Paris, the City of Flowers, love was no more to him than the sensation of a gentle wind caressing his cheek. To him, Edith Good was a fleeting spring breeze that passed in front of him.

Once, Gozo was making a sculpture of Edith, the daughter of a friend of Mrs. MacMonnies. She sat posing for him on a chair, and while he was working and during breaks in his work, they enjoyed a continual conversation.

At one point, Edith asked him in a roundabout way what he thought was the most appropriate way to express one's love for someone. He answered, "Probably with a kiss," at which point Edith replied, "Well, let me kiss you then." However, Mrs. MacMonnies was always around the place where Gozo was working, so he told her, "Maybe another time," and let the opportunity pass.

In his heart, Gozo regretted this. He really enjoyed being with the lovely Edith. What's more, Edith was going to return soon to the United States. In a few days he would probably be finished with his sculpture of her. On the one hand, they were both in a hurry to finish the sculpture, but he wished that the large studio was much smaller, a more intimate space where the two of them could be alone together.

One day, when there were only a few days left before they would have to say good-bye, Gozo was at last alone with Edith in the studio. She said to him, "This is an expression of my love for you," and kissed Gozo. They embraced each other. Although they only had a short time together, Gozo felt that it had taken them a long time to arrive at this moment. Edith said, "Please come and work in America. Don't worry about a salary. I can pay you. I have enough money to support you."

Gozo knew that she was speaking the truth. But he also understood the situation well. Edith's love was no more than the pure, sweet fantasy of a young girl. At some point, reality would set in, and her feelings, as fragile as cotton candy, would fade away.

So he told her, "Make sure you come back to Paris sometime," and he held her for a long time. The two never saw each other again.

Only the preparatory drawing he had made of her for the sculpture remained, and with it, some sweet memories.

After a while, Mrs. MacMonnies, who had been watching over the two of them, no longer mentioned Edith's name.

Shortly afterward, when he was working on a bust sculpture of a young woman called Margaret Draper, Gozo was starting to think of leaving Paris for a while and visiting another country.

But at the same time, he was telling his friend Harry in New York how beautiful Paris was in the spring, how blue the sky was, and how clear the air. He told Harry that he must come and see it. His enthusiastic praise of the city made Gozo smile bitterly.

One day, Gozo had gone out to the tennis courts with MacMonnies and his wife. The three of them were looking very sharp in their white pants and matching jackets. He noticed his own stylish appearance with great pride and realized that he was in the prime of his youth, a feeling that he would never forget as he grew older.

That same day, they ran into Bourdelle, Rodin's top apprentice. This was only their second meeting since the one at Rodin's salon. While they were talking, Gozo and MacMonnies realized that Bourdelle knew of the good work that Gozo was doing with MacMonnies and that he already considered Gozo to be a friendly rival.

After this, MacMonnies gave Gozo some time off. His friend Harry came from New York to visit him, and together they traveled to Rome. As they walked around the city and visited museums together, Harry completely relied on Gozo to take him around.

One evening when they were back in Paris, Gozo suggested to Harry that they visit a brothel, but Harry said that it sounded scary and that he didn't want to go, so Gozo left him in the hotel and reluctantly went out by himself into the city at night. After a short walk, Gozo reached a building at a certain street corner and went in through its small front door.

When he went upstairs, he came to a small room. He went inside and said a few words in French to the people inside. They seemed to understand him. He only had a few francs in his pocket, but that seemed to be enough, and he was able to get what he had come for.

When Gozo returned to the hotel and related a bit about his experience, Harry said that he wished he'd gone along with him. Gozo had never been to a place like that before then and never went again. He didn't regret going, but he never again felt the urge to go somewhere like that.

Exactly one year earlier, Gozo had been hospitalized and had had surgery for a hernia. Because he had found the nurse looking after him very attractive, he hadn't found his time in the hospital unpleasant. He enjoyed the way that she washed his back so much that he would have been happy to stay in the hospital longer than two weeks. We often hear stories of male patients falling in love with their nurses, but we rarely hear of this love fully developing.

Popularity with Girls

Gozo wondered to himself if he was a flirt or a womanizer.

He didn't think he was. Women certainly seemed to like him. But he was never the one who made the first move. But just like an insect looking for nectar in flowers, he went from one woman to another, so he realized he probably was a bit of a player.

The Life of a Sculptor: Gozo Kawamura

Gozo had invited Ferry, a woman he liked who worked at MacMonnies's atelier in Paris, to go to Rome with him. Since she hadn't been able to go, he invited her to join him at the villa in Giverny.

When Ferry arrived, the two embraced each other and cried, happy to see each other again after such a long separation. This time, Gozo really believed he was in love with her and planned to spend the night with her. It was an exceptionally quiet autumn evening.

When Gozo was closing the door of the main building, Ferry complained that she thought that something was moving outside. In Paris, the autumn leaves had already turned and were on the ground. The large trees at the MacMonnies's villa were also starting to lose their leaves.

It was completely dark outside.

When he held his breath to listen carefully, he was sure he could hear the faint sound of someone breathing.

If he'd been alone at night in a situation like this, Gozo probably would have screamed. But tonight Ferry was with him. He had to be brave and protect her.

Gozo grabbed an umbrella and held it like a club as he walked forward carefully on the fallen leaves, trying his best not to make a sound. Suddenly a large dog, Othello came leaping toward him.

Gozo and Ferry heaved a sigh of relief and returned to the main house. Soon everything was silent again. All they could hear was the sound of the light rain softly falling on the dead leaves in the darkness of the garden.

But then Ferry said, "Gozo, I just heard the window opening in the guesthouse."

"Really?"

"I'm sure I heard it."

Gozo tensed up again.

He stared hard into the darkness. Something was definitely fleeing out there. Gozo threw off the clothes he'd been wearing since Paris and put on his work clothes. In his hand he carried a gun.

Ferry lit a lamp and walked behind Gozo.

After a while, Gozo heard a sound, and then he saw what was definitely the shadow of a person. Ferry was gripping the left side of Gozo's white work coverall. She was trembling all over. Her fearful state reminded Gozo of a scene from a novel, and without thinking, he kissed her.

Then, with his gun in his right hand and his left arm around his girlfriend, he moved quietly toward the sound. He didn't want to hurt anyone with his important right hand. He didn't even want to get the hand he worked with dirty, but in this kind of situation, it was likely that whoever was out there had a gun too, so he gripped his gun tightly.

The guesthouse window was definitely open. He stared hard, and once his eyes got used to the darkness, he could make out the figure of a man. When the man saw Gozo, he ran off through the open front gate and escaped into the darkness. The man looked a bit like someone Gozo knew to be keen on Ferry. But he chose not to tell Ferry this. Out of a samurai-like sympathy for the other man, he wanted to protect his honor, but he wondered if the other man would realize his generous action.

By the end of the year, despite beginning with such a thrilling romance, Gozo and Ferry's relationship had faded without a trace. Gozo had broken up with Edith and with Ferry. One day as he sat alone in his atelier, he was overwhelmed by helplessness and sadness, feeling a great emptiness in his heart.

He wondered if he had really loved those two women. He probably hadn't. They seemed more like scenes in his imagination, like those in a dream.

He had already been living in Paris for two years. He was interested in going to London and visiting the national museums and galleries there, so he asked MacMonnies for his advice. MacMonnies agreed immediately that it would be a great idea.

However, when Gozo actually went to London, he felt like just another tourist there, which wasn't much fun. Perhaps Paris was better after all, he thought. But since he'd traveled all the way to London, he diligently sketched the streets there.

When he returned to Paris toward the end of 1911, he lived alone at the villa in Giverny, but this time he didn't feel lonely. Mr. and Mrs.

MacMonnies spent New Year's with him, and for Christmas they gave him a pocket watch, a gift that he remembered for the rest of his life.

The three of them went back to Paris and stayed at their main house. The MacMonnies often accompanied Gozo to the École des Beaux-Arts, and they often took him to eat at famous restaurants. They really loved Gozo, and he was very aware of this affection.

When they returned to the countryside, Gozo began working on a bust sculpture of Margaret Draper. She always assumed her pose very quietly, and sometimes when their eyes met, her cheeks would turn red.

Gozo had vowed to give up cigarettes and romance, but when he looked into her kind eyes, he started feeling that it was going to be hard to keep the latter vow. But he told himself that she was just another girl, and bathing in Margaret's gaze, he tried his best to focus on his work.

The Joy of Youth

Around this time, Gozo had fallen in love with a woman called Julie. When he and Julie went for walks in the rain, Gozo felt that he was in the springtime of his life; his heart was so full of happiness that he felt it would burst out of his chest. And when Julie wore her pale blue princess-style dress, she was so beautiful that he could hardly breathe. He wondered at the fact that some people could be born so beautiful.

Before Julie visited his atelier, Gozo had made many sketches of her from memory, but he thought that if he could draw her real body, the sketch would be really beautiful.

Whenever she came downstairs, he would hold her tight and kiss her. Even though she was wealthy, she wasn't in the least bit selfish, and one could even go so far as to say that she had the unaffected manner of someone raised in the country. She was interested in fashion, so she blended in with Paris life, but she wasn't poisoned by life in the large city. Since Gozo had already met Julie, who behaved appropriately for the pure, virginal girl that she was, he could not respond to the passionate gaze of Margaret.

Gozo spoke with Julie every evening without losing interest in her. Being able to spend his evenings with such a beautiful woman was so wonderful that he sometimes felt there must be some kind of mistake. With good luck like this, he felt that he had been granted a wonderful gift from heaven. He believed that a perfect beauty such as hers should be preserved for the future.

Her beauty was so delicate that even though Gozo was able to express an individual's unique beauty in his artwork, he doubted he could capture hers.

He wondered where Julie was from. She wasn't white. Her skin was brown, as if from a tan, and its texture was fine and silken.

Julie had told him her grandfather was from Hungary, and her mother was apparently part Mongolian or some other East Asian lineage. Her father was Jewish. To Gozo she was a perfect goddess created by the mixing of the blood of many diverse peoples. Gozo believed that he had to preserve her purity, and while they were together, he kept that promise. But this goddess disappeared from Gozo's life too.

From then on, Gozo became fearful of beauty. No longer would Julie kiss him goodnight. No longer would he see her sitting next to him working quietly on her sewing. Joyful memories of her floated back into his mind one after another.

Shortly afterward, new models came to his studio to sit for a new work. They were two American sisters. These rich girls had money to spare and had sought out this Asian artist. The older sister, Andrea, was always very talkative, even when she was posing for him. After working with her, Gozo would take her out for an hour to Montmartre, have dinner with her, and then drive her back to their hotel. No matter how passionately she kissed him, he told himself he would not go beyond being friends with her, Andrea's passion gradually excited him.

But according to his friend Harry, Andrea was engaged to one of his friends. Even though he didn't want to become embroiled in a love triangle, every Sunday would find him standing in front of his model Andrea.

He knew that if he didn't finish the sculpture as quickly as possible, he would become, as she would say, her prisoner. When she couldn't

The Life of a Sculptor: Gozo Kawamura

come, he threw himself into reading books and preparing his work for school, whatever it took for him to stop thinking about her.

One night, Gozo had a dream. He was running out of oxygen and having difficulty breathing, so he was breathing in oxygen from a pump. Andrea came and started kissing him, and although he shouldn't have been able to breathe because Andrea was blocking his mouth, he didn't feel any pain. In his dream, he was wondering why, when suddenly he woke up.

In the end, Gozo was able to end his relationship with Andrea without feeling too lonely.

Gozo could see the River Seine from the window of his atelier in Paris. The river always appeared full enough to burst its banks, and it flowed slowly along. The green trees along its banks looked lively, as if they had been inserted into the blueness of the sky. The morning mist would lift like a stage curtain to reveal the streets of Paris lit up in the morning sun. Gozo was always struck by the beauty of this scene.

Nature was more beautiful than love. Eventually the sun would rise and light up the city. Gozo's sentimentality would disappear like the morning mist, and in the light of the sun, he would be able to see reality again.

Then, just after Gozo returned from Italy, the MacMonnies suggested that he go to Germany, and he followed their advice.

At first, thinking he'd do some sightseeing in Germany and Denmark, he took a ride in a tourist carriage. The guide was a young American woman. She wore a white flannel outfit and a Panama hat and was quite lovely. When he looked at her closely, he noticed her eyes were narrow, almond shaped, and curved upward slightly.

The guide didn't seem to mind Gozo staring at her; she seemed just as interested in him. Perhaps because Gozo could speak English, she let down her guard, and when they rode under some cherry trees, she stopped the carriage, picked a cherry blossom, and gave it to him. Thanks to her, he was able to spend one of his sightseeing days completely happy.

While in Germany, he made a sketch of a bronze statue of Bismarck, with the intention of showing it to MacMonnies on his return.

When he was on the train from Luxembourg back to Paris, a group of young girls called out all at once, "You must be the Japanese sculptor who lives in Giverny!" They were a group of rich American girls who were studying at the École des Beaux-Arts.

On graduation day, Gozo met the group of girls again and was struck by how upbeat and fun they were. When he returned to Giverny, he had a mountain of studying to do to prepare for the École des Beaux-Arts preliminary exams. He read books on draftsmanship and architecture, and he translated anatomy texts into French and then translated French into English; it took a great amount of effort. Exhausted by the workload, he wondered whether he'd be able to pass the exams. He was so focused on his work that rumors started circulating that Gozo was strange and that he had gone off women, but Gozo knew this wasn't true; this was just a temporary state.

Around that time, two girls showed up at his atelier. Betty and Marjorie came on bicycles to play tennis. MacMonnies and the housekeeper from the villa had gathered at the tennis courts. The housekeeper, Lilly, couldn't play tennis, but she stood at MacMonnies's side in the sun working as his attendant.

Gozo's partner was Marjorie.

Once, Betty and Marjorie, who were sisters, had come with their father for an evening meal, and afterward Gozo had walked the three of them home as far as the train station. When Betty saw her younger sister laughing merrily with Gozo, she was happy inside. She knew that her sister liked Gozo. Their father didn't know what was so funny, but they all laughed together. Who knows what people thought when they saw the four of them walking along the streets laughing!

When the summer came, the two sisters returned to Paris, but they told Gozo that their friends Marcelle and Laura would be coming soon from Paris for a visit. Gozo grew impatient waiting and went to the gate to look for them a number of times. When the two women arrived, Gozo took them for drives and played tennis with them, enjoying the height of summer with them both. In their red knit shirts and white pants, the girls were a charming sight.

When they got back to the villa, they all tried their hands at making ice cream. When they tasted their creation, they squealed with delight at how delicious it was, and then declared merrily that they wanted to eat melon too.

The Life of a Sculptor: Gozo Kawamura

When you are young, you can have this kind of fun, without a care for others.

Top left: Study of a nude woman looking to the side, practice sketch, about 1913 (D)
Top right: Study of a nude man from behind, practice sketch, about 1913 (D)
Bottom: The Rodin Museum 2015, with a statue of *The Thinker* (from Google)

Seven

Return to New York (Age Twenty-nine)

The Challenge of Large-Scale Works

On April 21, 1913, Gozo received notification that he had passed his Scholarship Student Exams at the École des Beaux-Arts. Around the same time, MacMonnies had just received a commission from the City of New York for a large-scale sculpture. For Gozo too, the next twenty or so years were to be a period in which he created major works that would define his legacy as an artist. Working with MacMonnies, starting with the completion in 1918 of a sculptural monument decorating the triumphal gate in New York's Washington Square, he was to create several large-scale sculptures.

Here, we will look in detail at the monuments the two sculptors created for New York City municipal buildings in 1922. One was the colossal fountain sculpture *Civic Virtue* in the front garden of New York City Hall, and the other was the commission for a sculpture to decorate the main entrance of the New York City Library. The mayor of New York City from 1918 to 1925, John F. Hylan was a great lover of sculpture. During his term as mayor, he wanted to build a memorial to celebrate the virtue of the citizens of New York. He knew that MacMonnies, who happened to be from Brooklyn, was a sculptor with a great reputation in the European sculpture world and selected him for the project. MacMonnies accepted

The Life of a Sculptor: Gozo Kawamura

the commission and began work, assisted by his senior apprentice Edwin Megargee and Gozo, who had by then graduated from the École des Beaux-Arts.

However, the design for the sculpture *Civic Virtue* became highly controversial. It was originally designed as a fountain statue. The problem was that it depicted a man standing on top of female figures, apparently stamping on them. There was an uproar among some critics who claimed that Gozo must have designed the image. They claimed, "The Japanese Mikado's sculptor is insulting American women. We won't stand for the Japanese attitude toward women." To the Americans who supported the women's rights movement, the placement of women in an inferior position to men was a move in the wrong direction.

At the same time in New York, there was some dark gossip circulating. Bribery was rampant among city assemblymen. The mayor came under attack for promising to clean up the politics in the city of New York, where the Mafia had become too powerful, and then building a bronze statue that was lacking in public spirit.

Those in favor of the statue claimed that the women depicted in the work were not good women but evil women. They argued that the man in the statue represented righteousness standing up to and conquering temptation, represented by these wicked women. The city assemblymen and businessmen who gave in to the seduction of Mafia violence and prostitution were too numerous to count. The voices of the supporters of the statue rose up and declared that now was the time to transform their corrupt society into an ideal society.

On March 3, 1913, five thousand American suffragettes had marched to the White House in Washington. This movement had spread quickly throughout the country. Supporters insisted that MacMonnies's statue was really an expression of female beauty. The fountain in New York wasn't depicting women kneeling before a man but instead showed women and men supporting each other. The design was approved, and work on the statue continued as originally planned.

Then, the *New York Times* decided to run a citizens' questionnaire asking registered voters whether they were for or against the sculpture.

Readers voted overwhelmingly in favor of the statue, agreeing that art could help cleanse the hearts of citizens. This vote represented a victory of the virtue of the citizens who attached a high value to art.

However, as the plans were moving forward, another problem arose for Gozo. In order to be eligible to work on government projects, workers had to either be American citizens or have resided in the United States for at least twenty years. MacMonnies and Megargee knew that if they lost Gozo, they wouldn't be able to complete the project because of the large scale of the statues.

Now, the city hall's statue *Civic Virtue* was supposed to measure six meters high, with a base measuring eight meters high. After completing the city hall fountain project, the team had already been hired to create two sculptures for the entrance to the New York City Library, a figure called *Philosophy* on the right side of the entrance and *Beauty* on the left. The plan was for both of these figures to be large works measuring at least seven meters high. Without Gozo and the enlarging machine that he had invented, they wouldn't be able to complete such large-scale works. Only Gozo knew how to control the machine.

MacMonnies had wanted to have Gozo Kawamura credited as a coproducer of the statues, but Gozo was not an American citizen. MacMonnies and Megargee felt terrible about this, but they were powerless to remove the large obstacle blocking Gozo's participation in the project.

But Gozo was determined to participate in their construction even if he couldn't have his name on the statues legally. MacMonnies had become his teacher and mentor when he arrived in France as an unknown student and had looked after him well; now Gozo wanted to give him his complete support. He also wanted to help Megargee. Megargee was a man of good character who obviously had been well brought up, and he and Gozo had a warm friendship that lasted after MacMonnies's death. Megargee's father was a diplomat who respected other cultures and always tried to understand foreigners. Perhaps because of his father's influence, Megargee's warm friendship had deeply touched Gozo's heart.

The Life of a Sculptor: Gozo Kawamura

Above: The statue *Civic Virtue*, originally displayed in front of the New York City Hall (photo taken at the Queensborough Park while under conservation). Height 6 m, base 8 m. Photo by Takeo Kaji

Below: The two statues *Beauty* and *Philosophy*, flanking the entrance to the New York Metropolitan Library. Height 7 m, completed 1922 (U)

These statues have been damaged over the years, but they can still be seen at the library today. (U)

Completing *Civic Virtue*

Passersby would stop in front of New York City Library to watch the progress being made on the sculpture. Of course, many specialists also crowded around to watch. Because it was larger than any previous sculpture, MacMonnies had some raw materials sent from Europe. The largest of these was the twenty-two-ton block of marble he had shipped all the way from Italy.

Finally, the day came for the *Civic Virtue* statue to be placed in front of the city hall. Acting as site foremen, Gozo and Megargee installed the various sculptural elements that they had sent from Paris. When the giant sculpture was transported quietly out of the studio to the site, even the faces of the assistants known as "studio boys" who were pushing the cart that carried the statue glowed with pride.

In 1922, MacMonnies, Megargee, and Gozo were deeply moved as they stood staring at the statue that they had managed to successfully install in the front garden of New York City Hall. The project was finally complete. It had taken them about eight years, slowed down by World War I, which had forced them to evacuate Paris and move to London. The original sculpture was certainly made by MacMonnies, but the final giant fountain sculpture was undoubtedly made possible by Gozo's enlargement technology. But on the list of names of its creators, Gozo's name was nowhere to be seen.

However, when MacMonnies received the payment of $2 million from the City of New York, he divided the money up three ways, so Gozo was paid for his work. This was the first large payment Gozo had ever received. At last he had realized his dream of working as an artist. His work had made money; his efforts had borne fruit.

Now, Gozo thought to himself, if he drank only water and nothing richer, how would he be able to sculpt a figure of a beautiful woman? Who could sculpt a statue of a heroic soldier on horseback while wearing ragged clothes? Gozo tied a silk scarf around his neck, put on some suede shoes, and faced his work. Abundance was the wellspring of Gozo's art. If this spring dried up, he wouldn't be able to create. Gozo had always felt

The Life of a Sculptor: Gozo Kawamura

this way, but having already lost his mother and father, he found it sad that he had never had the money with which to honor them.

Love was also borne out of a bubbling spring. Without love, there naturally can be no tomorrow. Edith and Margaret, whose company he had enjoyed in Paris, both lived in New York, but his feelings for them couldn't be called love. With them, he was doing nothing more than playing with fire.

Gozo, who had been away from New York for three years while studying, found that New York had a very different energy from Paris. While he had been working on the commissions, he had reconnected with some of his friends from the National Academy, and this excited him. His friends had heard rumors about Gozo and MacMonnies and Rodin, and dividing into two groups, the MacMonnies fans and the Rodin fans bombarded him with questions about each artist. They all understood that he had experienced something that rarely happens, something one only dreams about, and they looked at him enviously.

They talked with him with such excitement that it would seem that they themselves were about to be interviewed by Rodin. Under the influence of alcohol, they sat around Gozo, saying whatever they wanted and laughing hard.

Very few people had the talent and good fortune that both Gozo and Megargee had. His friends understood well enough the mystery of lucky encounters, and they wondered if and when they too would have such luck.

Twenty years later, in 1941, because New York City Hall underwent an expansion, the fountain sculpture *Civic Virtue*, which Gozo and his fellow artists had created, was moved to a new location in Kew Gardens, Queens, west of the Borough Hall. Today, the legacy of these American artists has tragically almost been destroyed by pollution. In 1997, when I went to New York and stood looking up at the statues *Philosophy* and *Beauty* at the New York City Library, I saw that after eighty years these statues too were severely damaged. The carved lines in the relief sculptures under the library building's eaves and the two statues on either side of the entrance could still be clearly seen, but over in Queens, the fountain statue that had been moved there no longer had running water, and the park's lake was completely empty too. The statue itself was stained by exhaust fumes, and the figures' faces all had broken noses. Their cheeks looked sunken, just like people who had grown old. It was as if these damaged sculptures were speaking of the tragedies that Gozo had lived through.

But the world is as kind as it is cruel.

Just before this book went to press, I learned of some good news. The City of New York is now working to repair the statue. When I told them that I was writing a biography of Gozo, the person in charge was pleased that he would now be able to learn something about Gozo's life, so I promised him a copy upon publication.

World War I

Let's go back in time a little. In 1913, Gozo received a medal for a clay model that he submitted to the École des Beaux-Arts, and then qualified as a scholarship student. Then, free to study what he wanted at the École des Beaux-Arts, Gozo was able to begin to map out a basic direction for his future. Armed with the conviction that he could study anywhere he wanted, he believed that he wouldn't even need a graduation certificate.

He went regularly to the Louvre Museum. One day, when he was making his way home alone from MacMonnies's studio, he cut through the Luxembourg Gardens, and through the soft early summer rain, the sound of the drum that announced the park gates were closing echoed through the air. The sound had the solemnity of music by Wagner, and when Gozo exited the park onto Boulevard Saint-Michel, he had a strange urge to go back into that solemn atmosphere.

The figure of Gozo walking through the rain holding a walking stick blended in perfectly with Paris. Gozo would never forget the mysterious scene of that evening.

The Life of a Sculptor: Gozo Kawamura

But the peace of that evening was to transform completely into chaos and confusion. World War I (1914–1918) was pressing closer and closer to the city of Paris. The German army had forced Belgian refugees to flee across the border into France. Antwerp was on the verge of surrendering before a fierce attack by the German army. King Albert, who led the Belgian army, was already escaping on a boat to England. Russia had sent an army of prisoners from Siberian prison camps to fight the Germans at the front. A feeling of unrest was building up moment by moment in Paris.

Even in the suburb of Giverny, where Gozo and his companions were staying, the tension of war was starting to rise. All French men between the ages of twenty and forty-eight were being enlisted, and only the old men were left behind. MacMonnies had offered his villa to the French government as a headquarters for the Red Cross, so people from the villages went there to volunteer as nurses to take care of injured soldiers. All the people there worked with all their hearts.

The war continued into 1915. That year, a German submarine sank the American passenger ship the RMS *Lusitania*, which was on its way from New York to Liverpool in England, killing 1,198 people. Because millionaire Alfred Vanderbilt, a close friend of the twenty-sixth US president, Theodore Roosevelt, was among those who died, former president Roosevelt criticized Germany, calling the attack "an act of piracy."

Then, when Germany started launching poison-gas attacks and enveloped Europe in fear, the United States sent its soldiers to the European front, turning the war in favor of Britain and France. The German forces began their retreat, and on November 30, 1918, they were finally defeated.

The MacMonnies and Gozo had evacuated briefly to Britain, and now they were able to return to France. Shortly after their return, they went to work on the *Civic Virtue* statue and the *Beauty* and *Philosophy* statues for the New York City Library using Gozo's enlarging machine, pouring all their energy into completing the marble statues.

MacMonnies's next large-scale commission was a memorial statue of the first US president, George Washington, commissioned by Princeton University to commemorate the Battle of Princeton in the American War of Independence. Completed on June 18, 1922, the statue of the country's first president stands at the entrance to the university. MacMonnies designated Gozo as the supervisor of this project. The statue was twelve meters high and eight meters wide, and it weighed more than forty tonns. The final giant statue is so splendid that photographs of Gozo working on it made him look even smaller than he already was.

I went to Princeton twice to see this statue, and of course after eighty or so years, the statue showed some signs of damage from snowstorms. Because it is on the campus of Princeton University, few cars pass it by, so it wasn't damaged by vibrations or exhaust fumes. It had fared better than the New York City Library statues, but it was still damaged, and it looked pitiful. After the publication of this book in Japanese, I was happy to learn that in 2006 to 2007, the statue underwent conservation.

Eventually, Gozo brought his new bride, Jeanie, from Paris to live in New York, and while the next ten years or so. It became an important time for him to record his name in America, these were also some of the most painful years of his life personally.

The Life of a Sculptor: Gozo Kawamura

The George Washington Battle Monument on the grounds of Princeton University. Height 8 m, completed June 18, 1922

Eight

Japanese Artists and Pioneers in the United States (Early Twentieth Century)

Gozo's Notable Forerunners

Until now, we have been looking at this period in time with a focus on Gozo Kawamura, but during Gozo's lifetime, Japanese artists were like infants on the world stage, not yet confident internationally. By the time when Gozo had been inspired by his distant relative Banka Maruyama to travel to the United States, many other Japanese people had already made the voyage to America.

In the 1890s, young artists aiming to travel to Europe typically made their first stop in the United States and stayed there for a few years before making their journey to France.

For example, Yoshio Markino (1869–1956) and Senko Kobayashi (1870–1911) stayed for a while in San Francisco, while artists like Kyohei Inukai (1886–1954) gradually moved their lives eastward. He spent three years in Hawaii before continuing on to San Francisco and enrolling at the Mark Hopkins Institute of Art (now the San Francisco Art Institute).

Around 1940, with rumors circulating about a possible war between Japan and the United States, when Gozo had returned home to Japan after an absence of thirty-six years, he found in his luggage a picture by Kyohei Inukai.

Set against a dark background was a woman wearing a hat and looking directly at the artist, with lips painted a pretty red. At the bottom right corner of the painting, he could read the faint signature INUKAI.

Those Japanese artists eventually left California, where anti-Japanese sentiment was strong; they traveled eastward to Chicago, Boston, and New York, and finding a more peaceful environment there, enthusiastically began their artistic activities again, studying and presenting their work.

In 1906, Kyoto artist Katsuji Makino came to New York with Yukihiko Shimotori. Around that time, a Japanese chemist called Jokichi Takamine had achieved fame worldwide for developing a stomach medicine called "Takadiastase," and he soon became a millionaire. Takamine, who entered New York's high society, had been encouraged by his wife, Caroline, to assemble a collection of paintings by James M. Whistler (1834–1903), himself a well-to-do impressionist who had been influenced by Japanese woodblock prints.

Sometime afterward, Katsuji Makino won the confidence of Takamine and was hired to design and furnish the interior of Takamine's New York mansion. For this project he collaborated with Seigoro Sawabe (1884–1964), a Nihonga artist of the Sumiyoshi lineage who had a passion for learning, and Eitaro Yoshida, who was aspiring to become an architect, and together they created a magnificent mansion.

After this Takamine had the idea to purchase from the Japanese government the Phoenix Hall, or Ho-O-Den (later renamed the Wind in the Pines Hall, or Sho-Fu-Den), the Japanese pavilion built for the 1904 St. Louis International Exposition. Makino worked with him to dismantle the pavilion and rebuild and renovate it on Takamine's estate. Today, at the Takamine Mansion, on the wall of the rebuilt Sho-Fu-Den, the mural painting of the Wind God and the Thunder God still remains brightly colored, with the signature KATSUJI written with a brush. Of all the Japanese artists working hard to make a living in New York, Makino certainly had the most enviable existence.

In 1905, Jokichi Takamine was worried that the anti-Japanese sentiment in California would spread across the country, so he established a Japan Club with himself as the sponsor. The club, which was created as a place where Japanese exchange students and workers could gather, still exists today as the Nippon Club.

The bacteriologist Hideyo Noguchi came here to play shogi, or Japanese chess. The artists Eitaro Ishigaki, Yasuo Kuniyoshi, Riichiro Kawashima, and Takeshiro Kanokogi also often stopped in at the club.

Araki Norio, who was a friend of Hideyo Noguchi later in his life, made the club his base while he studied American advanced dental technology. In his late years, he made advances in Japanese dental treatment, and he is renowned for his many achievements. He was also a long-time friend of Gozo Kawamura's and kept in touch with his wife, Shiori, even after Gozo died.

Japanese Artists Who Moved in Various Directions

In 1917, Ryusaku Tsunoda entered Columbia University. At that time, the only courses relating to Japan in American universities were about Japanese art, and there was no institute where students could research Japanese language or culture. Lamenting this state of affairs, Tsunoda returned to Japan and gathered several tens of thousands of books about Japanese culture. He brought them back to the United States with him and established the Center for the Study of Japanese Culture at Columbia University, leaving a great legacy of achievement.

Lois Johnson, who was later to become Gozo's assistant, had studied Japanese art and culture at this center.

Ryusaku Tsunoda's name was on Gozo's Christmas-card list. It is unclear whether Gozo's relationship with Tsunoda predated Lois's relationship with him, but either way, it is certain that the three of them were connected. It seems that Tsunoda had a high opinion of Gozo's talent. Later, when Gozo returned to Japan, Tsunoda gave him a letter of

The Life of a Sculptor: Gozo Kawamura

introduction to journalist and historian Soho Tokutomi and sent him to Tokutomi's house. This was a fruitful introduction, as Gozo's first commission when he returned to Japan was to create a bust sculpture of Tokutomi.

One unique character was Kango Takamura. He went to work for Paramount Studios in New York and then worked in Hollywood, Los Angeles, but when the United States went to war with Japan, he was sent to an internment camp. After the war, he moved back to Los Angeles and then worked for many more years in Hollywood. In his later years, he became a devout Christian in the Anglican Church, and because of his easygoing character, he was much loved among the Japanese American community. Despite his colorful history, everyone in his community would call out, "Hi there, Mr. Takamura!" and have a warm conversation with him. He was also a skilled archer who worked as the accountant for the Los Angeles Kyudo Kai (Los Angeles Archery Association).

Toyo Miyatake was the foremost Japanese American photographer. When Japanese Americans mentioned photography, they thought first of Miyatake, and everyone believed that photographs commissioned from his studio in Little Tokyo were the best. He had been the exclusive photographer for Japanese butoh dancer Michio Ito in Hollywood, and his subtle photographic skills have withstood the test of time. Although Miyatake only received commissions from a small group of people, he went out with his son, Archie, to take photographs outside the studio. His wife, Hiroko, was well known for being an elegant beauty. When Toyo died in February 1979 at the age of eighty-three, his funeral was held at the hall of the Koya-san Temple, and two thousand people came to pay their respects and lament his passing.

Toyo Miyatake's teacher had been Harry Shigeta, who happened to be from the same village as Gozo, Usuda in Nagano Prefecture. His photography has also been highly acclaimed in the United States.

At around the same time, Isamu Noguchi was already gaining considerable attention. As is well known, Noguchi became hugely successful in a very short time, and in his later years, he was invited by the

Segerstroms, the great farming family from Orange County, California, to create sculptures symbolizing the lima beans that had made the family so rich and to design a garden for the sculptures. I attended the opening ceremony for the garden, and I remember fondly Isamu Noguchi signing a gold fan for me. And everyone knows about his sculpture for the Nagasaki Atomic Bomb Memorial.

Later, the Isamu Noguchi Plaza was created in front of the Japanese American Community and Cultural Center in Los Angeles. As a square that celebrates the mutual understanding between Japan and the United States, it is continuing to carve out new history today. Also, Nisei Week, a Japanese American Festival that began in Los Angeles in 1939 in connection with Noguchi, has been held in Little Tokyo every August for over sixty years, except during World War II.

I met the renowned artist Sueo Serizawa once in 1958, when we were introduced by Reverend Kataki of the Los Angeles Holiness Church. At that time I was about to make my way home from the church, when Serizawa kindly offered me a ride, and the three of us drove together.

Even though I had the opportunity to meet these famous people, I wasn't very knowledgeable at the time, so I undoubtedly missed some once-in-a-lifetime chances to get to know these people better. Now I am embarrassed that I stayed so quiet with them and didn't show enough interest or respect. Even though Reverend Kataki told me, "You should take a look at Mr. Serizawa's paintings," I never went to see them, and in the end I only saw them after Serizawa passed away.

In 1903, Chiura Obata (1885–1975) enrolled at the Mark Hopkins Institute of Art in San Francisco, California, along with Kyohei Inukai. During World War II, while he was interned at the Topaz War Relocation Center in Utah, he made many sketches, and after he was released, they were exhibited in San Francisco and Los Angeles.

However, in the 1930s, when anti-Japanese sentiment was mounting, there had been an increasingly strong movement to ban the works of Japanese artists from exhibitions, so Yasuo Kuniyoshi, Ura Obatachi, and Henry Sugimoto vehemently protested against this injustice.

The Life of a Sculptor: Gozo Kawamura

On December 8, 1941, when the news was broadcast that Japan had attacked Pearl Harbor, the greatest fear among the Japanese living in the United States became a reality.

Those Japanese residing in Los Angeles who held positions of leadership, such as employees of the chamber of commerce and heads of Japanese prefectural associations in the United States, were arrested that day.

Without even being asked to show their identification documents, these first-generation Japanese Americans were immediately locked up in state jails, all the while protesting, "What's going on?"

Although the police told them to be patient for a little longer, the next day they loaded about one hundred of them onto trucks used for transporting convicts and drove them to Terminal Island, near Long Beach. Once there, officials told them, "Don't worry. We guarantee you'll be safe." Then the order went out for all Japanese American families to leave their homes.

Allowed to bring only belongings they could carry in their hands, mothers couldn't hold their children's hands. American soldiers apparently felt sorry for them and tried to help them, but they didn't tell the women where they were going or what had happened to their husbands who had already been taken away, so the women were extremely anxious.

Eventually, they were all assigned to a number of relocation camps throughout the United States. They were sent out to the deserts of Utah, Arkansas, New Mexico, and Arizona. Nisei (second generation) Japanese American lawyers and executives protested to the US government that these Japanese Americans were American citizens, some of them second generation, and that it was unfair to treat them as if they were the enemy.

Many Nisei Americans swore a pledge of allegiance to the United States, and in order to protect their families, they volunteered to go to Europe and the Pacific to fight for the United States.

Within the relocation camps, there were two factions among fellow Japanese Americans: those who thought Japan would win the war, and those who thought Japan would lose. Fighting broke out between them, causing hysteria throughout the camps.

Young Issei (first generation) Japanese Americans and those who had been to college started schools inside the camps and began teaching English and math.

Because of the attack on Pearl Harbor, those Issei Japanese Americans, who had recently come to the United States with nothing to build a new life, lost all of their property and confidence they had built in the United States.

One Issei poet wrote:

Toraware no mado ni haruhi no sashikomite
Nodokani ato wo ba kakomu hito ari

Rays of spring sun pour through the prison window
People stand in them, wrapped in calm.

For some of the hard-working Japanese American pioneers, it was hard to deny the fact that they were experiencing tranquility for the first time in their lives in the camps.

Some Nisei artists were able to continue their oil painting while in the camps.

When it started to become clear that the Japanese were going to lose the war, some prisoners were released from the camp before the war ended. There were some who returned to their original homes, while others moved to the East Coast in search of a new home.

Japanese American Artists Who Were Sent to War Relocation Centers (Internment Camps)

Chiura Obata (1885–1975): Topaz, Utah
Miné Okubo (1912–2001): Topaz, Utah
George Matsusaburo Hibi (1886–1947): Topaz, Utah
Henry Sugimoto (1901–1990): Rohwer, Arkansas
Toyo Miyatake (1895–1979): Manzanar, California

The Life of a Sculptor: Gozo Kawamura

Kango Takamura (1895–1990): Santa Fe, New Mexico
Isamu Noguchi (1904–1988): Poston, Arizona
Shiro Kamiyama (1889–1954): Manzanar, California
Jack Matsuoka (1925–2013): Salinas, California, and Poston, Arizona

> Enlisted in the US Army and enrolled in the army's language school. Received training in military intelligence, communication, and interpretation

Miki Hayakawa (1904–1953): Santa Fe, New Mexico
Charles Erabu "Suiko" Mikami (1901–2012): Topaz, Utah
Taneyuki Dan Harada (1923–1983): Tanforan Assembly Center, California, and Topaz, Utah
Matsumi "Mike" Kanemitsu (1922–1992): held in a series of detention camps

> Enlisted in the 442 Unit of the US Army and was sent to the European front in 1942

Matsumi Kanemitsu, who had studied with Yasuo Kuniyoshi, was barely known in Japan, compared with in the American art world, and it wasn't until 1998, fifty years after the end of World War II, that the National Museum of Art in Osaka held the first Japanese retrospective exhibition of his work.

"In art, there are no national borders." This is simply official language. Anti-Japanese groups wouldn't let Japanese American artists join American art organizations, thus preventing the great artists among them from rising to prominence.

In the 1910s, when Gozo Kawamura was working on the building of the American Press Center, Japanese and other foreign artists were not permitted to participate as artistic advisers, and many of the bronze and clay sculptures that Gozo worked on and delivered as a collaborator were officially credited to MacMonnies.

This demonstrated the huge importance of citizenship as a foundation for life in the United States, a country of immigrants. This is still the case today; in fact, nowadays immigration laws are even stricter. This is an issue, not of cultural divisions, but instead of political trust. A person who is not a US citizen cannot be hired by any government organization at the federal, state, or city level. But on the other hand, doors are open to becoming a naturalized citizen.

A provision of the Federal Art Project established in 1935 called for the revision of the law that prevented many artists from participating in cultural projects because they were not US citizens.

The difficulties faced by Japanese American artists during this period became a thing of the past after the end of World War II. Since then, it is truly gratifying that today, the high level of Japanese artists has been acknowledged worldwide.

Left: Sculpture of an angel under construction, to be displayed at Radio City Music Hall along with the work of Yasuo Kuniyoshi, completed 1916
Right: Sketch of Jeanie Farque, who Gozo married on August 12, 1916 U

Nine

Marriage and Divorce (Age Thirty-two)

Marrying Jeanie Farque

After the prototypes for the sculptures for the New York City Hall fountain and the Municipal Library reliefs of *Beauty* and *Philosophy* were completed and Gozo had used his enlarging machine to make the final large-scale sculptures, he returned to Giverny still full of excitement and passion.

When he went into the atelier, he found Jeanie Farque, who had been training to be MacMonnies's studio assistant while Gozo was still in Paris. The room was dark and very cold, and she was sitting with her legs stretched out in front of her, warming her feet in front of the fireplace. Jeanie, who had been waiting in France for Gozo for a long time while he was in New York, appeared lovelier than ever to him, and he embraced her tightly. Gozo's bed in the studio was only big enough for one person, but Jeanie refused to go back to her hotel. After such a long time, Gozo was happy that he wouldn't have to walk her home at night and then sleep in the studio alone. So that night, Gozo and Jeanie made love over and over again in the narrow bed. Then, exhausted, they both fell into a deep sleep until morning.

From that day, their relationship was very intimate. Jeanie was a student at art school, but she always made time to drop by Gozo's studio and help with the plaster casting, and soon all the sculptors working in the studio came to consider her a treasure. Gozo himself was drunk on the happiness he felt from being able to spend all day working with the woman he loved. He became captivated by the charms of her blue eyes and her full figure. Gozo had fallen for many women, but those women's looks all paled in comparison to Jeanie's beauty. Gozo, who had fallen in the twinkling of an eye for her intensity, soon found himself trapped, paralyzed inside a fortress called marriage.

Gozo drove the 120 km round trip from MacMonnies's main house in Paris to the villa in Giverny. When he arrived at the villa, Jeanie, who had been waiting for him, arranged chairs in one corner of the studio, made Gozo lie down, and then showered him with kisses. They then got drunk and fell asleep right there. When they awoke, they remembered their evening and laughed together.

However, MacMonnies brushed aside the women who surrounded Gozo, and he didn't approve of Jeanie, who seemed overconfident that she was going to win Gozo's love. Mrs. MacMonnies also had a hunch deep down inside that Jeanie's love was dangerous and that Gozo should not accept it.

But Gozo was so blind with love that he couldn't imagine that this lovely young flower, who had just turned twenty, had been sprinkling poisonous pollen all around her.

On August 12, 1916, Gozo and Jeanie were married and received their marriage certificate from the Consulate-General in New York. Gozo registered their marriage at the town hall of his hometown, Usuda, so Jeanie was able to become a Japanese citizen, a fact that remains in the records today. Jeanie was born November 6, 1892, the eldest daughter to a French family named Farque. She became a Japanese citizen, but nothing else is known about her other than the fact that her father was a colonel in the French army.

An Unhappy Married Life

After two years or so, Jeanie, who might have been spoiled as a child, began to lose her loveliness, and she behaved selfishly toward Gozo. She began ordering him around.

"Gozo, you don't have to work so hard. We have enough money now."
"Gozo, that model isn't great; you should get someone else!"
"Gozo, don't leave me alone. I'll end up going off somewhere."
"Gozo, did you kiss that model?"
She developed a jealousy that grew worse by the day.

Sometimes at dinnertime, Jeanie would complain so much that Gozo couldn't bear it; he would get up and flee into his studio. There, he would take out his anger by kicking the base of the sculpture he was working on until he calmed down.

Once when she saw an upright sculpture of her that he was working on, Jeanie asked him, "Who's this?"

When he replied, "It's you," she exclaimed, "That's not me! You used someone else as a model. Who on earth is it? Tell me her name!" She urged him so jealously to tell him who it was that he shrank back in fear.

In the end, one day Jeanie hit the sculpture so hard that she put a dent in it.

On another occasion, Gozo was so caught up in a sculpture he was making of a dancing girl that Jeanie kicked that one too. It was hard for him to get any work done.

At around that time, MacMonnies had received the commission to work on the large pieces in New York. Gozo was keen to get to the United States as soon as possible. He thought that some time apart would help them cool down so that they could repair their relationship if it was possible.

But one day, Jeanie's beloved cats were making strange whining sounds because it was mating season. The unpleasant sounds were irritating Gozo, so he picked up his pistol and fired it once in the air to scare the cats. Jeanie screamed, "You're a murderer! You're a murderer!" and burst into hysterical tears.

On another day, Jeanie wanted to go dancing and asked Gozo when he would be coming back home from the studio. He thought it might be good for her if they sometimes went out together, so he told her, "I'll be ready soon."

But she replied, "I want to go right now!" and left without him.

That night Jeanie came home late and was wiping her mouth vigorously with a handkerchief. "A horrid man kissed me. It feels disgusting," she said and spat so that Gozo could see her. Gozo could see through her story and knew she was making it up.

On another occasion, a female model was coming to the studio, so Jeanie suggested that they all eat dinner together, but then she quickly changed her clothes and went out. That evening she didn't return home until late.

Gozo had an idea about who she was meeting when she went out, but he realized he needed to confirm his suspicions. Gozo had heard rumors that she was seeing a young Frenchman, so he was very concerned about this young man. However, one day when he said to her, "This evening I'll come out with you," she replied with a very cool expression, "Don't worry, I'm meeting a group of girls this evening."

On Christmas Eve, Gozo was invited to the annual party organized by a group of artists at a hotel. Usually Gozo went with Jeanie, but this year she said she that wasn't feeling well and that she would stay at home. On his way out, he told her that if he came home late, he would sleep in the studio, but he left the party early. When he got home, Jeanie wasn't there; she had gone out. Gozo was aware that she was up to something. He waited for her to come home as if he knew nothing. At three thirty in the morning, Jeanie came home with a young man and brought him inside. After a while, Gozo quietly sneaked into her room and saw them intertwined on the bed.

The next morning, Gozo asked her, "Who was that man last night?"

She answered, "That was just a friend. But if you don't believe me, maybe we should get a divorce," and she took $200 spending money from Gozo and headed out again.

The Life of a Sculptor: Gozo Kawamura

Gozo's assistant, Harlen, saw these exchanges between him and Jeanie and said to Gozo, "Jeanie is a bad woman. She's a liar, and she's unfaithful to you."

Harlen had been working for Gozo for the last year as a studio assistant and secretary. She was a very quiet woman, so it was surprising to hear such strong words come from her mouth. As a husband, it is never pleasant to hear someone speak badly about one's wife, but Gozo couldn't bring himself to defend Jeanie.

Jeanie was also jealous of Harlen. Harlen was very wise, and she did various jobs for Gozo without letting Jeanie's harassment bother her. Her concern for him made him happy, and he considered her a good friend.

The statue of George Washington that Gozo and MacMonnies had been working on together for the War of Independence memorial was complete, and they had sent the marble prototype and its base to the United States. Because they now needed to use Gozo's enlargement machine to create the final work, Gozo would have to travel to the United States.

Jeanie said that she wanted to go too. Knowing that Jeanie could be a very hard worker and thinking that going together to the United States might give them a break from their jealous fights and bring them closer together again, Gozo agreed.

The statue at Princeton is twelve meters high and eight meters wide, a giant work that one can only look up at.

Gozo was unrivalled in his use of the technology of the enlargement machine. The enlargements he made had exactly the same proportions as the original in both the three-dimensionality of the overall form and the precision of the details.

On June 23, 1922, the *New York Times* reported, "The ceremony to unveil the new War of Independence Memorial Statue was held with President Harding present. The statue depicting the 1st Pennsylvania Regiment and the 1st Maryland Regiment was designed by Frederick MacMonnies."

The name Gozo Kawamura was nowhere in the article.

When it came to credit for the statues, Gozo obediently followed the laws of the United States and accepted his role as MacMonnies's invisible assistant.

The art world was certainly not ignoring Gozo; it recognized the artistic collaboration between MacMonnies and Gozo.

Jeanie didn't care that Gozo's name wasn't on the statue. She knew that, as was the case in New York, Gozo would be receiving one-third of the $2 million production fee for the statue. It was at this point that she began to plan to divorce Gozo.

In the third year after they had married, Gozo decided to divorce Jeanie, and they separated. But the full-blown divorce proceedings with Jeanie were to maintain a stranglehold on Gozo for thirteen years after the separation. Beyond the divorce settlement money itself, Jeanie had arranged for Gozo to pay her continuous alimony.

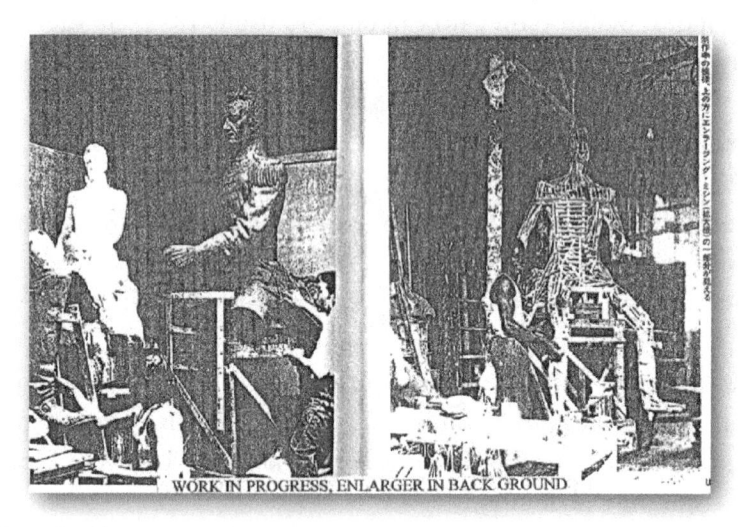

Left: Gozo looking over at the prototype made of plaster over a wooden skeleton as he completes the final statue (U)

Right: We see part of a sculpture enlarging machine during production in the upper section of this picture.

Gozo Creates His Masterpiece, *The Ideal Bull*

During that time, fortunately for Gozo, he was able to leave New York and throw himself into his work. This was thanks to an invitation from a Minnesota dairy farmer named Fred Pabst Jr., who also happened to be the president of the Pabst Beer Company.

Pabst wanted to produce superior cows that could compete with European breeds, so he commissioned Gozo to create bronze sculptures of a cow with an ideal body shape. His plan was to reproduce this sculpture many times and donate the copies to the The Holstein-Friesian Association of America and agricultural universities. Gozo made calculations from his understanding of anatomy and designed an imaginary cow. He created two hundred models of this ideal cow in bronze.

Pabst treated Gozo as a first-class artist. He set up a cow research center and studio for him on a farm in Texas and sponsored his long-term stay there. Here, Gozo went beyond the world of sculpture. He immersed himself in the zoology of selective breeding, wondering if the ideal cow could be produced by cross-breeding Jersey cows with Holstein cows. He spent many months and years focused on research into selective breeding.

On June 6, 1922, the *Kansas Chronicle* reported that the sculpture of a cow made by Gozo Kawamura, a resident of New York, had been examined by the Judging Committee of the Holstein-Friesian Association of America. The newspaper reported that Gozo's sculpture, which measured twelve inches in height and two feet in length, received many questions and requests from the association members.

Gozo told them that there was no more perfect Holstein cow than his model, and with these words, his work was finished.

On June 5, Gozo, who was staying in the Baltimore Hotel in Kansas City, received news from the Judging Committee that his model and Edwin Megargee's painting of a cow had won the top prize for "The Perfect Holstein Cow."

This was actually a story of great patience. It took a total of six years from the time Fred Pabst first contacted Gozo in 1916 to the day Gozo completed the statue in 1922.

The newspaper *American Agriculture* wrote the following account:

The superb collaboration of Gozo and Megargee has resulted in the creation of an image of the ideal cow, unlike anything that has ever been created before. As a result, the sons and daughters of dairy farmers all over the United States, who own a total of 500,000 heads of Holstein and Friesian cattle, will produce more and more of these ideal cattle.

Without agriculture, this country would not flourish. Future generations of American dairy farmers will attain this ideal for sure.

Both the brilliant sculptor Gozo Kawamura and the painter Edwin Megargee were beloved students of Frederick MacMonnies, who was considered modern America's most exemplary artist.

This large project took them many years, but it became the foundation for the extremely rapid development of America's dairy agriculture. In the near future, Americans would be able to drink delicious milk and eat tasty steaks.

From the country's expansive pastures, fodder for the animals was transported all over the country via railroads, and then by trucks to each farm. New train lines had to be laid, and these lines had to be maintained.

Not only the dairy farmers were affected; these innovations were a huge benefit to the whole American economy.

A Cleveland newspaper reported the following on June 5, 1923:

We have created images of our ideal cow. Gozo Kawamura, a Japanese sculptor who lives in New York, is particularly well known for his animal sculptures, but he also collaborated with Frederick MacMonnies to create the statue Civic Virtue. *Gozo studied at New York's Academy of Design and then at the Ecole des Beaux Arts in Paris.*

> *Gozo handled dissatisfaction and requests with great patience, and working from his studies of anatomy, faithfully expressed the living form of the cow. His perseverance can be felt in the very form of the cow he created.*
>
> *The cow created by Gozo Kawamura will from now be the standard with which America's cows will be judged at agricultural fairs. The cows that have been bred to look the most like his will undoubtedly win first prize.*

Thus, Gozo became known as "Gozo of the Cow" not only in the United States but also among dairy farmers in Europe.

Moreover, President Calvin Coolidge (who was President Harding's vice president but was sworn in as the thirtieth American president after Harding's death from an illness in August 1923) also heard about Gozo and commissioned a bust from him. From November 1924 to January 1925, a number of letters came to Gozo from the White House, one of which was signed by the president himself.

If he could create such a splendid cow, he could surely create a sculpture of the president. Gozo's reputation had now attained its highest point.

Fred Pabst, who had supported Gozo in US, was apparently unaware that Gozo had returned to Japan in 1940 and then had created a bust of General MacArthur after the war. However, Pabst did learn of Gozo's death, and as a way of memorializing Gozo, he went to great efforts to have his sculpture of MacArthur brought back to the United States.

In this way Pabst, who had discovered Gozo, made sure that Gozo did not disappear from the view of his admirers, even after his death.

Pabst was deeply moved that the "Gozo of the Cow" of thirty-six years before had returned once more to the United States.

Jeanie was endlessly spending the money she was extracting from Gozo. She hired a powerful Jewish lawyer and steadily built her case against Gozo for the divorce settlement. She eventually attained a substantial settlement from Gozo. Their divorce was finalized in court on July 10, 1935. It took nine years to settle Jeanie's suit. It is said that she won $1 million dollars from him (in 1930, $1 was worth 2 yen; at today's rate of $1=100 yen, that sum would be equivalent to 100 million yen). Because Gozo and Jeanie shared a bank account, whenever Gozo received payment for a work of art, Jeanie knew exactly how much he had earned. In this way, Jeanie was able to take most of Gozo's fortune.

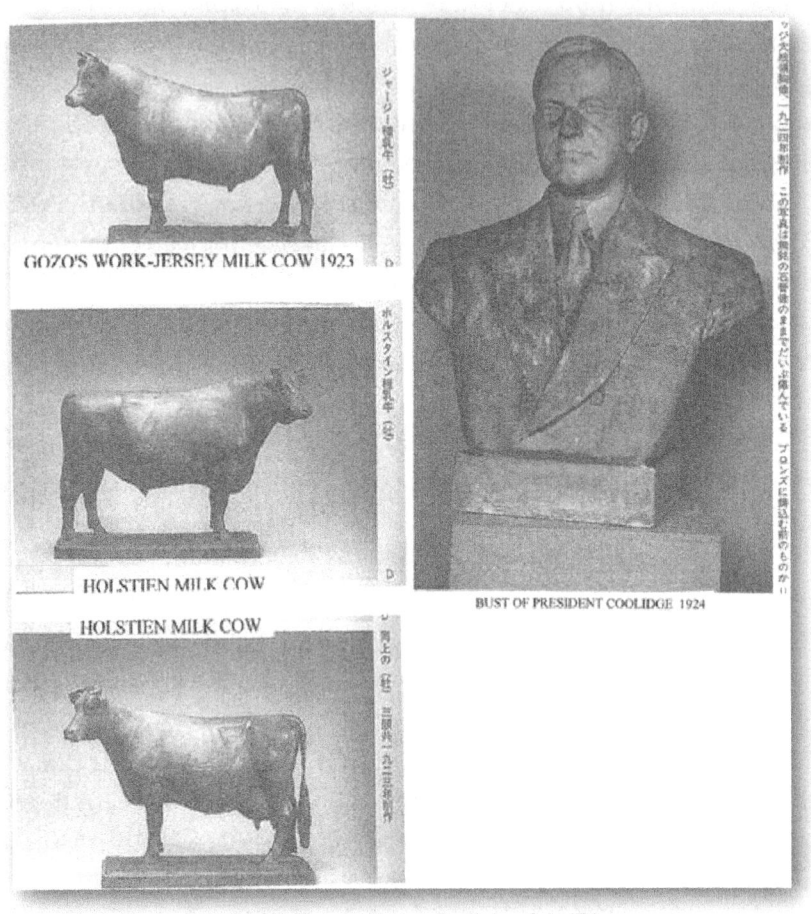

Left top: Jersey Dairy Bull (male) (D)
Center: Holstein Dairy Bull (male) (D)
Bottom: Holstein Dairy Cow (female) (D) All three figures were made in 1923.
Right: Bust of US President Calvin Coolidge, 1924. The photograph is of an unsigned plaster model that shows some damage. This was probably a prototype that was later copied in bronze. (U)

Ten

Shiori and Waka Yamada (Age Fifty-five)

Marrying His Better Half

Gozo lost his fortune to Jeanie, but eventually he was free from years of bitter struggle, and he felt his load lightened. However, perhaps because of the shock of the legal and financial battles, his health had deteriorated considerably, and he was admitted to a hospital in New York, where he was forced to look after his body and mind. But to Gozo, who had been running since he had landed in the United States over thirty years before, this was a welcome rest.

One day, while he was in the hospital, his friend Tamotsu Minowa introduced him to a Japanese woman who could chat with him so he wouldn't become lonely. Her name was Shiori Maeno.

Gozo, who hadn't spoken with a Japanese woman for a very long time, found her much more emotionally calm than Western women. It was probably a cultural difference. When they talked, they found they had endless interests in common. When they discussed food, Japanese foods like sweet red-bean paste and New Year rice cakes came up in the conversation, and his nostalgia for them calmed his heart.

Perhaps because of these chats, he eventually recovered his health. Even after returning home, he kept seeing Shiori. Then, on March 30, 1939, Gozo married Shiori in Woodbury, Connecticut, with the New

York consul general of Japan, Kaname Wakasugi, and Reverend Giichi Kawamata serving as witnesses.

Gozo was fifty-five, and Shiori was thirty-six years old.

Shiori had been married before to a man called Fujio Maeno (whose father, Yoshizo, was a wealthy member of the Lower House from Osaka), and at the same time she had established the Kinka Koto Dressmaking School in the Nishi Sugamo District of Tokyo. However, her husband had died suddenly from influenza, and she was left to look after their five daughters.

Yoshizo Maeda encouraged Shiori to manage the school for the sake of her and his granddaughters' future.

Kinka Koto Dressmaking School had the following organizational structure:

Principal and Dress Designer: Shiori Maeno
Advisory Committee:
    Member of the House of Lords, Yoshiharu Tadokoro
Principal of the Joint Girls' Professional Training School, Haruko Hatoyama
    Japan University Professor, Yuzo Kaneko

Shiori managed the girls' professional training school with advisers like Professor William Clark and Motomichi Miwada, but she also ran the school as a creative educational organization that provided young women, particularly those from rural areas, with the professional knowledge, skills, and encouragement they needed to become independent. In addition, she opened her home to deaf students and provided full-time instruction for twenty of them.

Shiori's work resonated strongly with the women's rights activist and commentator Waka Yamada, who contacted Shiori on October 14, 1939, and invited her to join the Women's Mission of Inspection to the United States that she was organizing.

By the way, one of my husband's relatives was a journalist by the name of Shigeki Oka. He and his wife managed a Japanese-language newspaper in San Francisco. In 1955, when I arrived in the United States with my husband, Seiko Iinuma, we immediately went to the Okas' house on Bush Street to pay a visit.

Shigeki Oka was a hot-blooded, zealous man. Not bothered by poverty, he argued heatedly with his aunt Toshi about Japanese American society. In October 1955, when my husband was a poor student studying engineering in Illinois, his family unexpectedly came to visit us in the tiny one-bedroom apartment in Chicago where we were living with our two children. At that time, Oka took us to eat at a Chinese restaurant on Clark Street. Since coming to the United States, our family had not gone out to eat at a restaurant. When he ordered some *hamuyu* (a small, salty fish) and told us how delicious it was, my husband chuckled. The hamuyu that arrived on a small plate was just salty, steamed fish. It was in fact the cheapest item on the menu. First-generation Japanese American laborers were proud of going out to eat *chop suey*, but that dish was only hamuyu and rice.

Shigeki Oka was also the person who helped the socialist Shusui Kotoku, who was from the same hometown in Tosa province (modern Kochi Prefecture), come to the United States. When Oka went back to his hometown, the special government secret police apparently followed him around. His nephew Shozo Oka and my husband, Seiko, were raised in Kochi like brothers, so even today they still call each other "older brother" and "Seibo." My husband is in his seventies now, and the only people who call him "Seibo" are members of the Oka family.

At that time, Uncle Oka, as we used to call him, was saying that he was planning to visit New York and Washington and then return to San Francisco. He said he wanted to investigate the condition of Japanese war brides. During the years 1952 to 1958, many Japanese women married American soldiers and came to the United States as war brides, but Uncle Oka said of the women who came to the United States, "They haven't changed a bit."

He knew that many of these war brides were already leading the lives of prostitutes in the bars of San Francisco. This is when he found out about Waka Yamada, who had been a prostitute but was now very active and well known as a social reformer.

Waka Yamada (born Waka Asaba) had a dark past working as a prostitute on the streets of Seattle and San Francisco.

According to Uncle Oka, who was a mine of information, when Waka Yamada came to the United States and gave her first speech, there was a lot of loud jeering.

Waka Yamada, though coming from such a background, was able to turn a new page of her life by marrying Kakichi Yamada. Waka Yamada recognized in Shiori wisdom and a strong ability to get things done and hoped that Shiori would become her successor.

Raicho Hiratsuka (1886–1971), a pioneer of the Japanese feminist movement, published a magazine called *Seito*, or *Bluestocking*, and instructed Japanese women about feminism. She devoted her life to fighting for women's right to vote. Waka Yamada, Sueko Otsuka (president of the Institute of Kimono), the wife of Tsuneo Matsudaira (previous Japanese ambassador to the United States), Chioko Azabu, Catherine Araki, and the wife of Ambassador Hiroshi Saito were all sympathizers.

Celebrated author Ogai Mori supported Raicho Hiratsuka. It is said that, years before when Ogai Mori was an exchange student in Germany, he had seen the liveliness of German women and felt sympathy for the first time for Japanese women, who were socially restrained.

Shiori was empowered by Waka Yamada's courageous lifestyle. She left her five daughters in Japan and traveled to the United States as part of the Women's Mission.

This was a major turning point in Shiori's life.

Shiori had a great sense of design for Western-style clothing, so no sooner had she set foot in the United States than she was inspired by the new fashion she saw around her. She would return to her room, stand in front of her mannequin and wrap cloth around it to figure out the structure of the clothing she had seen in the streets. Eventually, she decided that she wanted to remain in the United States alone and study fashion, so she parted company with Waka Yamada and left for New York to research Western dressmaking and clothing and accessory design. She arranged to have three of her five daughters, who were still in Japan, adopted individually into the households of her own brothers and sisters.

The Life of a Sculptor: Gozo Kawamura

Only her eldest daughter, Sachiko, and her fourth daughter, Reiko, remained officially her daughters, whom she would raise herself, but while she was in the United States, she arranged for them to live with relatives.

In the photograph taken of Shiori and Waka Yamada in front of the Diet Building in Washington, DC. Shiori is the one wearing Western-style clothing (while Yamada is in kimono). However, after meeting Gozo, she left the world of clothing and accessories behind to help him in his studio, and she was barely recognizable from before in her work clothes.

Left: Commemorative photograph from a visit to the White House, December 7, 1937. From the right: Shiori Maeno, Waka Yamada, and their interpreter. (U)
Photograph courtesy of Junko Sato
Right top: Gozo (age 55) and Shiori (age 36), both marrying for the second time (U)
Right bottom: Shiori (third from the right), Gozo (center), and Yasuo Kuniyoshi (far left) (U)

Shiori's Ability Blossoms

When Shiori started helping Gozo with his sculpture, a talent that had been hidden within her began to manifest itself. She was able to help Gozo produce his work by climbing nimbly up on top of his large models, which measured 1.8 meter in height, and work on the upper sections following instructions from Gozo, who stood down below. She was a perfect assistant. By marrying Shiori, Gozo had truly gained a better half, as they say. And Shiori looked very young, not at all like the mother of five daughters.

It was 1939 when Gozo married Shiori. At that time, he was working on a sculpture of celestial dancers for the entrance to the Japanese Pavilion in the New York International Exposition, so they had to postpone their honeymoon. The work was a two-panel relief sculpture measuring a total of eight meters high and six meters across.

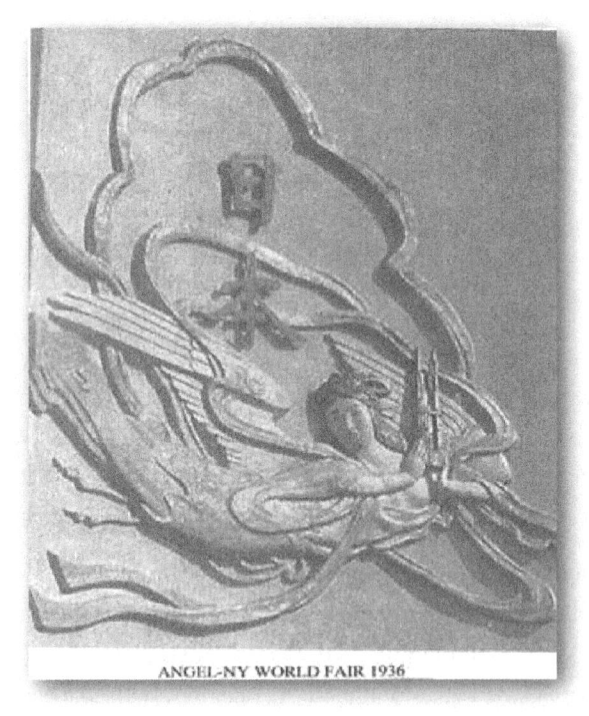

One panel of a two-panel relief sculpture of *Celestial Dancers* at the entrance to the Japanese Pavilion at the New York International Exposition, 1936. The panels were removed after the exposition ended, so only a photograph remains. (U)

The Life of a Sculptor: Gozo Kawamura

At that time, many Japanese artists were being brought over to create works for the International Exposition. Isamu Noguchi was hired by Ford Motors to design a fountain for their section, while Yasuo Kuniyoshi, Fuji Nakamizo, and others were creating works to show in a modern-art exhibition.

Visitors to New York could visit the Washington Square Arch and see the two majestic sculptures on either side and the relief sculptures that covered the whole arch at Washington Square. Completed in 1918, these sculptures were also Gozo's work. When the poet and novelist Toson Shimazaki, who was from the same town as Gozo, visited New York on his way home from Brazil, he called on Gozo. When they stood together looking up at the arch, Toson said, "This makes me very happy!" The two men would meet again in Europe some years later, but for now Toson was also delighted because Gozo had become recognized as MacMonnies's collaborator on this work.

Shortly afterward, when Banka Maruyama visited Paris, he met Gozo for the second time. Seeing how successful Gozo had become, he cried with happiness and told Gozo that he would tell his family back in Nagano about him when he went back to Japan.

Around that time, Gozo, who had not only laid his roots down overseas but had become very successful, was feeling very far away from his place of birth. And because of Shiori, he had reached the end of his journey in search of love.

As an extra note, before Shiori married Gozo, she had been working for businessman and art collector Kojiro Matsukata. She was on a research trip for Matsukata, observing the social circumstances of various countries, including, of course, the United States but also Germany and Czechoslovakia. While on this trip, she met Helen Keller, and this meeting resulted in Gozo's creation of a bronze bust of her later, in 1949.

While Shiori was on her trip, Gozo felt the same bittersweet longing that he had felt once before in Paris. He noted in his journal, "Since my beloved Shiori went to Chicago, I have felt really sure about our love for the first time. Shiori, please come back as quickly as you can and show me your beautiful smiling face. I know I will never think about another woman again." It was as if he had regained his youth.

Gozo happily agreed to adopt the two daughters Shiori had officially kept as her own. "I have never had children of my own, so suddenly having two daughters has made me unbelievably happy!" It was hearing these words from Gozo that convinced Shiori to marry him. In 1940, when Gozo and Shiori returned to Japan, they changed Sachiko and Reiko's names from Maeno to Kawamura. Now Gozo had a family of four people. Thanks to Shiori, Gozo was able to look forward to a peaceful later life.

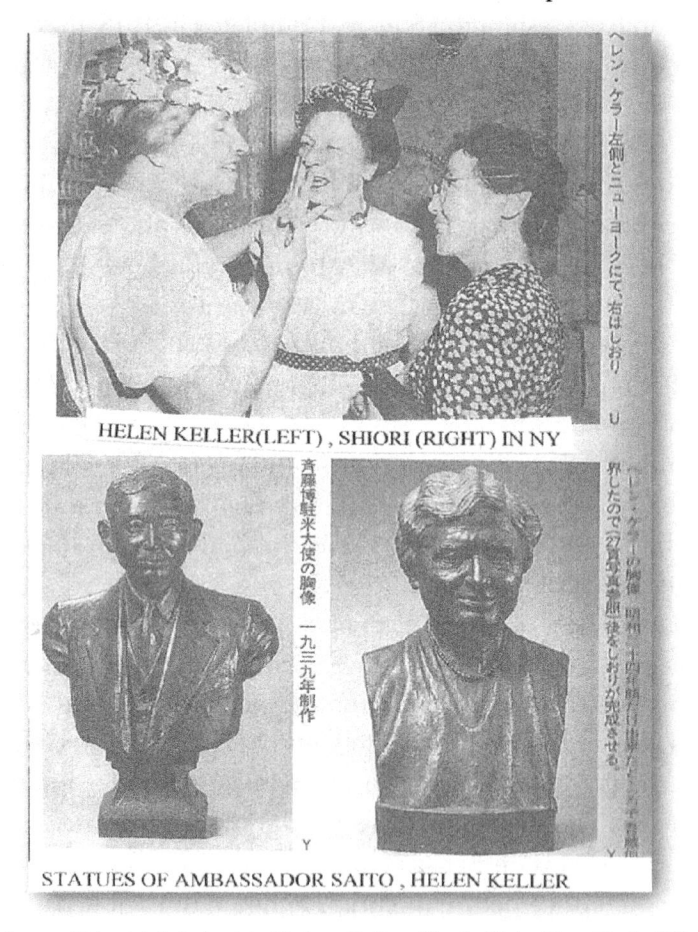

Above: Shiori (right) with Helen Keller (far left) in New York (U)
Below left: Bust of Ambassador Hiroshi Saito, 1939 (Y)
Below right: Bust of Helen Keller. The statue was unfinished when Gozo died in 1950, so it was completed by Shiori. (Y)

The Life of a Sculptor: Gozo Kawamura

TRIUMPH GATE , NY WASHINGTON SQUARE　　1918

STATUES AT NY CITY LIBRARY BY GOZO

Top: The statues and relief sculptures on the Washington
Square Arch, New York, 1918 (R)
Bottom: Statue by Gozo at NY City Library

Returning to Japan after Thirty-Six Years

In 1939, as US-Japan relations were deteriorating, Japan's ambassador to the United States, Hiroshi Saito (1886–1939), strongly recommended to Gozo that he return to Japan. Having been away from Japan for so many years, Gozo was anxious about how much his country would have changed and how he would be received there now.

He was very close to Ambassador Saito. Saito had complete faith in Gozo and Shiori, and they felt great respect and affection toward him. Shiori, in particular, had been friends with Saito even before Gozo. After he made the suggestion, she said, "Well, if Ambassador Saito thinks we should go back..." and immediately started making preparations to return to Japan.

While they were making preparations, Ambassador Saito, who they loved and respected, fell ill and passed away. Kensuke Horinouchi was appointed as the next Japanese ambassador to the United States. On the advice of New York consul general Kaname Wakasugi, Gozo decided to return to Japan.

In 1940, Gozo was asked to submit his work to an exhibition to celebrate the 2600th anniversary of Japan's Imperial era. Gozo was considering creating a sculpture of Professor Hideyo Noguchi, who died while working as a researcher for the Rockefeller Institute of Medical Research, and a sculpture commemorating the achievements of Ambassador Hiroshi Saito, who had participated in the first general meeting of the League of Nations, the Washington Naval Conference (1921–1922), and other historic gatherings. Gozo chose to express his passion and his hope of relieving some of the tension between Japan and the United States in his typical gentle way, by deciding to return to his home country.

But did Gozo really want to return to Japan? In Tokyo and Usuda, would he feel oppressed?

Would Gozo, who had from his younger days become used to the dynamism of American life and the refined character of French life, be able to adapt to life in Japan in the midst of war, which he truly detested?

Shiori also had to think hard. She had left her five daughters behind in Japan and remarried in the United States. Would her daughters and other family members welcome her back warmly when she returned home?

In the midst of their wavering, neither Gozo nor Shiori could imagine receiving a grand reception back in Japan during such a difficult political time.

Gozo wondered at the mysterious nature of life and at the irony of having left Japan to avoid the army and now returning when it was in the midst of a great war.

Eleven

Gozo's Friends (First Half of the Twentieth Century)

Toson Shimazaki, Hideyo Noguchi, and Others

In New York's Japan Club, there were many Japanese pioneers. These people were to be the driving force behind the birth and prosperity of modern literature, painting, science, and medicine in the late nineteenth and early twentieth century in Japan.

Toson Shimazaki (1872–1943)

Bust of Toson Shimazaki, 1943 (D)

From Nagano Prefecture like Gozo, poet and novelist Toson Shimazaki created celebrated publications, including *Transgression* (Japanese: *Hakai*), *Before Dawn* (Japanese: *Yoakemae*) and *Spring* (Japanese: *Haru*). Shimazaki had based the characters for his book *The Watercolor Painter* (Japanese: *Suisai Gaka*) on Gozo's distant relatives Banka Maruyama and Kiyoko Yamamoto, who then entered into a dispute with the publisher, Chuokoronsha.

The Life of a Sculptor: Gozo Kawamura

Gozo often met Toson when the latter was on one of his many trips to Europe and the United States. When Toson came to Paris, he visited Gozo. At that time, Europe was under attack from Germany. Not only Parisians, but also the refugees who had poured into France from the neighboring Netherlands and Belgium, were in a state of chaos and confusion.

Gozo wanted to make sure Toson was safe, so he found him a place to hide in the ceramic producing town of Limoges in the south of France.

Toson was grateful to Gozo. Before, there had been some tension between them because he had used Maruyama as a model in his novel, but now there was no longer ill feeling between Gozo and Toson.

Gozo made a statue of Toson, which to this day is displayed at the Toson Memorial Museum in Komoro City, Nagano.

HIDEYO NOGUCHI (1876–1928)

The year before he set off from the Rockefeller Institute of Medical Research to Accra in Africa to research the cause of yellow fever, Gozo had earned a commission via the artist Takeshiro Kanakogi, from Fukuoka Prefecture, to create a sculpture of Noguchi. Apparently, Noguchi hadn't liked the sculpture that Russian sculptor Sergey Konenkov had created of him because it had depicted his distress in too fine detail.

Bust of Hideyo Noguchi, 1939 (D)

Gozo created a sculpture that depicted Noguchi with a softer expression that conveyed the wisdom of his later years. Later, Noguchi sent Gozo a letter saying how grateful and happy he was with the sculpture and included with it a gift of dental floss, which was little known to the Japanese at that time. Gozo and Noguchi are said to have played Japanese checkers (go) together at the Japan Club in New York.

Gozo's statue of Noguchi is on display at the Hideyo Noguchi Memorial Museum in Inawashiro in Fukuoka Prefecture.

KYOHEI INUKAI (1886–1954)

In 1900, Inukai left Japan and traveled to Hawaii to stay with one of his relatives. In 1903, he moved to the mainland of the United States, to California, and enrolled in the Mark Hopkins Institute of Art (now the San Francisco Art Institute). In 1906, he visited the Chicago Institute of Art on his way to New York. Gozo and Inukai both joined the Gachoukai, a club formed by Japanese artists living in New York, and became good friends.

Kyohei Inukai and Gozo Kawamura did not become good friends only because they both had Western wives; they also appear to have had similar personalities. They were both elegant men who had suffered hard times but had come through them cheerfully. As a portrait painter, Inukai associated with many upper-class women, just as Gozo did as a sculptor. Inukai, like Gozo, took a very academic approach to his work.

Inukai's wife and Gozo's wife, Jeanie, both went to art school. Even though she didn't meddle in Inukai's work, his wife, who was from a wealthy family, was very selfish. The couple had three children, and although they appeared to have the perfect international marriage, they ended it after ten years.

Inukai died in 1954, four years after Gozo's death.

Sadly, very few of Inukai's works are known today. Perhaps this is the fate of portrait artists, or maybe many works have survived but are hidden in private collections. Gozo had one work by Inukai, which he kept until he died.

In contrast, Gozo kept many of his bust sculptures, from the original plaster models to the replicas that he kept to preserve a record of the works he had cast in bronze. These works by Gozo were donated to the Cultural Center in his hometown of Usuda in Nagano, where they are kept safely on display. (Another fourteen works were donated to the City of Yokosuka in Kanagawa Prefecture.) When I learned that the Shinano

Art Museum in Nagano Prefecture was planning to hold an exhibition entitled "50 Years After his Death: The Works of Gozo Kawamura" from February 18 to March 28, 2000, I was deeply moved.

Professor Jokichi Takamine (1858–1922)

Jokichi Takamine was a scientist best known for isolating the enzyme Takadiastase and the hormone adrenaline and then becoming rich by controlling their production rights. He was had a very close friendship with Hideyo Noguchi.

When Takamine was dying, his wife, Caroline, asked Gozo to make his death mask. In 1995, almost seventy years after Takamine's death, Kawamura's family donated this death mask to the Great People of Kanazawa Memorial Museum in the City of Kanazawa.

Kentaro Katakura (1849–1917)

Kentaro Katakura II was also from Nagano Prefecture. He learned silk spinning from his father Kentaro Katakura I, who ran a silk-thread-producing business. Katakura II became famous throughout the world as the "Silk Emperor" and was considered a hero in the Japanese silk industry. From 1922 to 1923, he traveled to Europe, North America, and South America on a research trip, and when he was in New York, he visited Gozo and commissioned a bust sculpture from him.

The sculpture was made of pure white marble and was beautifully finished.

Bust of Kentaro Katakura, May 1930 (Now in the Katakura Museum)

Out of all of Gozo's sculptures currently in Japan, this is the only white marble sculpture, and it is unique. The piece is dated May 1930, so Gozo must have spent a long time working on it while he lived in New York.

Now this bust sculpture can be seen at the Katakura-kan Mansion in Suwa City. When Kentaro was on his research tour, he was very impressed by the abundance of social welfare organizations in rural regions, and when he returned to Japan, he constructed a large hot-spring bathhouse—the Katakura-kan Mansion in Suwa City near Lake Suwa—and opened it to the public. When I went to Suwa to look for Gozo's sculpture, finding this wonderful bathhouse was a real bonus. It was as if Gozo was telling me, "Well done finding this place! Now please spend the day resting your bones here in the bath."

YOSHIHARU TADOKORO (1871–1927)

Yoshiharu Tadokoro was an education expert who had served as secretary of the Ministry of Cultural Affairs, commissioner of Gakushuin University and the Imperial Household Department, and a member of the House of Lords. He was an early supporter of Gozo. Coincidentally, Tadokoro had been one of Shiori's advisers when she was principal of the Kinka Koto Dressmaking School. In 1942, Gozo created a bust sculpture of Tadokoro.

YUKIO OZAKI (1858–1954)

Yukio Ozaki (also known by his pen name, Gakudo Ozaki) was a politician who served sixty-three years in Japan's House of Representatives and is remembered as the "Father of the Japanese Constitution." Gozo worked on a bust sculpture of him when Ozaki was ninety-two. Apparently, Ozaki admired Gozo's detailed preliminary drawing and was very pleased with the final sculpture. In his book, *The Collected Papers of Yukio Ozaki*, Ozaki made the following comments about the experience:

> *Shiori, the wife of Kawamura Gozo, the sculptor who made the bust of this old man, visited me with a photograph of the sculpture. Gozo, who was born much later than me, had died before finishing the bust beyond the neck point, so his widow Shiori showed up wearing a ski jacket and told me she had completed the sculpture, as a "husband-wife collaboration." He laughed at saying, "It's too good!" and explained the reason why of all the statues lined up in the Diet building of the successive generations*

of Heads of the House of Representatives, only the one of "old man Yukio" has no decoration.

In Japan, there was no one else who could make a statue like this of me. Even the statues of Itagaki Taisuke, Okuma Shigenobu and Ito Hirobumi leave something to be desired. The Japanese aren't very good at making bronze sculptures. I didn't want to have a sculpture made of me that would put our country to shame.

(From the "The Collected Papers of Yukio Ozaki," Volume 10, page 724.)

This elderly politician had consistently advocated for world peace and for constitutional government, which Japan had created seventy years before in 1890 by establishing its National Diet. For these reasons, Ozaki was a "World Treasure," and the truth of this could be seen in the eyes of this sculpture made by Gozo Kawamura.

HOSHIRO MITSUNAGA (1866–1949)

From his time as a correspondent for the *Asahi Shimbun* in Osaka, Mitsunaga was a big player in the world of Japanese journalism. Before others, he understood the synergy between news and advertising and established both a news agency and an advertising agency, Nippon Kokoku Kabushiki Kaisha (Japan Advertising Ltd.). He eventually merged the two agencies into Nippon Dempo Tsushin-sha (Japan Telegraphic Communication Co., Ltd.), or "Dentsu." However, the Japanese government introduced regulations that forced the separation of advertising and news, so he focused on advertising, and Dentsu grew into Japan's largest advertising agency and one of the three largest in the world. Mitsunaga was an adviser for the Gozo Kawamura Support Association.

ENKU UNO (1885–1949)

Enku Uno was a folk-religion scholar. He admired the roughly cut sculpture of the Buddhist sculptor Enku. Uno was an adviser for the Gozo Kawamura Support Association.

Soho Tokutomi (1863–1957)

Soho Tokutomi and his younger brother, Roka Tokutomi, were two major literary figures of the Meiji (1868–1912) and Taisho (1912–1926) periods. He published newspapers and magazines including *Nippon no Shorai* (the *Future of Japan*) and *Kokumin Shimbun* (the *People's Newspaper*). His most significant achievement as a historian was *Kinsei Nihon Kokumin shi* (*A History of Early Modern Japan*), which was published in one hundred volumes.

Gozo's first sculptural commission after he returned to Japan was a bust sculpture of Tokutomi. I discovered the following letter written to Tokutomi about Gozo:

> Dear Mr. Tokutomi,
> *I apologize for not being in contact for so long.*
> *May our honorable nation continue to grow robust and prosperous.*
> *Mr. Gozo Kawamura is a sculptor originally from Shinano (Nagano). After living in Paris he moved to New York, and he has not only excelled among his fellow Japanese artists, but his work is considered outstanding even among American and European artists. I have been a friend of his for twenty years.*
> *He has a sincere character.*
> *He has returned to his home country to create images of the New Japan, which is part of the new order in East Asia. As Japanese men who wish to commemorate the New Japan, both you and Mitsuru Toyama should preserve your images for posterity. Gozo Kawamura shares your feeling about Japan, so when he returns to Japan, I hope that you will give him an audience and will allow him and his wife to create a sculpture of you.*
> *With this letter, I am introducing you to Mr. Gozo Kawamura.*
> *October 14, Showa 15 (1940)*
> *Columbia University Library,*
> *Japanese Collection, Ryusaku Tsunoda*

When Ryusaku Tsunoda heard the news that Gozo was returning to Japan, he wrote this letter of introduction and delivered it personally. Apparently, he always carried letters personally to Soho Tokutomi.

The Life of a Sculptor: Gozo Kawamura

This is how Gozo began his relations with Soho Tokutomi.

When Tokutomi saw the completed bust sculpture, he was so happy he declared the work to be "superhuman skill" and made efforts to establish a Gozo Kawamura Support Association. Today the statue is displayed at the Tokutomi Soho Memorial Museum in the town of Ninomiya in Kanagawa Prefecture.

When I went to find this statue, I found not only the bust of Tokutomi but also the letter of introduction from Tsunoda and a total of seven hand-written letters from Gozo stored in their records. There was also a rolled-up letter written with a brush and a typed text. In addition, I discovered from a conversation with the museum's curator, Shizuko Kono, that there should be a pair of bust statues of Mr. and Mrs. Tokutomi in the Ochanomizu Library in Tokyo.

When I inquired there, they did indeed have the statues.

In the Ochanomizu Library, in the Seikido Bunko (a special library for women in the Chiyoda District of Tokyo), carefully stored in the basement were the two statues—one of Soho wearing Western clothing with a necktie and the other of his wife, Shizuko, in Japanese dress.

A plaque on the stand bore Gozo's seal, the date March 15, Imperial Year 2602 or Showa 17 (1942), and the inscription "Presented by the Japanese Newspaper Association." The statue of Tokutomi at the museum had been completed on August 12, 2601 (1941), so presumably because Soho had admired Gozo's "superhuman skill" so much that the Japanese Newspaper Association commissioned Gozo to create statues of Tokutomi and his wife as a gift to them.

Nonetheless, it seemed that I was the first person to inquire about and photograph the statues at the Ochanomizu Library. Since the statues had not been looked at or touched for over fifty years, there was not a single trace of dirt on them.

After finishing the statues, Gozo became friends with the Tokutomis. During the Occupation, when food was scarce, Gozo took some of the food he received from the occupying forces to the Tokutomis' home. From Mrs. Tokutomi, Gozo received letters of thanks, which also reported on her husband's condition.

Nobuko Iinuma

Establishment of the Gozo Kawamura Support Association

In June 1944, the Gozo Kawamura Support Association was established. It had its headquarters in an office on the fifth floor of the Marunouchi Kaijo Building in Kojimachi, Tokyo. Its prospectus reads as follows:

Prospectus for the Sculptor Gozo Kawamura's Support Association

Gozo Kawamura, a member of the American National Sculptors, lived overseas for 37 years, worked hard studying at national art schools in France and the United States, graduated from the sculpture department with special commendation from the Chancellor.

Since then, through his devotion to research, his diligence in research, his focus, he has created highly unique works of art that radiate elegance, purity and spirit and received high acclaim in Europe and the United States. Now, today, the name of Gozo Kawamura is gaining wider recognition.

To commemorate the year 2600 of the Imperial calendar, he returned to his home country and has remained silent for a year. As the sole sculptor of this Imperial nation, he has worked diligently with self-consciousness and self-discipline. But, some time ago, in a studio in Kyodo in Setagaya, he was working on a bust sculpture of Prince Fushimi-no-miya Hiroshi-O, and when he was completing it, he received as many as two visits from prince himself at the studio.

Furthermore, when he made the bust sculpture of Soho Tokutomi, he was so inspired by Kawamura's "supernatural power" that he picked up a brush and composed a whole-hearted letter of gratitude and appreciation.

We are establishing this organization with the hope of introducing the high quality work of Gozo Kawamura to a wider audience in Japan, and we ask you all for your comments and support. We hope that with everyone's support, the artist will be encouraged, his passionate sculpture will attain the devotion of the country. It is our sincerest hope that his art will contribute to the elevation of this Imperial nation's culture.

As advisers, the club had members of the House of Lords Soho Tokutomi, Yoshiharu Tadokoro, and Hoshiro Mitsunaga and Japan Academy member Enku Uno. In addition, there were twenty-five members who joined as sponsors from the industry and news world.

TSUGUHARU FOUJITA (1886–1968)

Awarded the *Légion d'honneur* from the government of France, Foujita was a Western-style, or *yoga*, artist, and the first Japanese artist to work in an international style. Later he became a French citizen and changed his name to Léonard.

He was also invited to join the Support Association, but he declined with the following note:

> *To Gozo Kawamura,*
>
> *I am afraid I have to decline your invitation to become a founder or supporter of your support association or to write recommendation letters to art associations. From now on, I am sorry but please do not use my name in relation to the club. I am firmly declining to be involved.*
>
> *You seem to have exaggerated things when you said there would be about two or three friends there. It was a large meeting and I didn't like it at all. I'm sorry to put it so directly but I hate it when so many people are lined up like that.*
>
> *As an old friend, I am asking you this out of friendship. Please only promote me when it comes to my military work for the Imperial Rule Assistance Organization.*
>
> *Please forgive my impoliteness.*
> *June 5 (The Day of a State Funeral)*
> *From Tsuguharu Foujita*

During the war, Foujita wanted to work with the Japanese army and navy as a military propaganda artist at the southern front, so on his own initiative he collaborated with the army to promote the war. Rather than being an artist who loved peace and pursued beauty, Foujita saw and portrayed some dreadful sights. His paintings, including *Final Fighting on Attu* and *The Fall of Singapore,* won him the Asahi Prize. Later he was criticized for supporting the war.

Four years after Japan lost the war, Foujita returned to France and became a French citizen. This type of self-transformation characterized his admirable way of life. One could say the same for Gozo, but although he seemed at first glance to have given up his integrity in order to survive the war, there was no compromising in his art. Rather, his works show that, during tense times, he polished his skills as an artist.

With the above exchange, Gozo's relationship with Foujita came to an end.

As for the Gozo Kawamura Support Association, with the worsening of the war, there was no room for such cultural activities.

Evacuation to Usuda, Shinshu

In 1944, the Americans were launching increasingly furious air attacks on the Japanese mainland. At that time, air defense practices were a regular occurrence in Kyodo in Setagayaku, where Gozo was living.

According to Gozo's journal, "a 20kg firebomb fell on Mr. Saito and Mr. Yonezawa's house. All evacuated. Serious chest injury. Left arm broken. Rescued one person. Put out the fire. Helped the neighborhood committee to put fires out." There were many pages filled with similar detailed notes.

They learned how to protect themselves from fire with wet straw mats and how to pour buckets of water correctly. Men supervised and made sure that the women wouldn't scream. They made sure they knew the faces of all the neighborhood children. They faithfully followed all the instructions for the wartime regime.

Meanwhile, Kawamura's family (namely Shiori and Sachiko) prepared to evacuate the city and head to Shinshu (Nagano).

The following items are what they planned to take:

The Life of a Sculptor: Gozo Kawamura

1. Modeling tool, 2. Plaster, 3. Carpentry tools (hammer, 2 electric saws, level, others), 4. Shoes, overcoat, underwear, handkerchiefs, scarf, other

Shiori's plan: 1. sewing machine, 2. Buddhist altar, 3. House shrine, 4. Radio, 5. Buy firewood, 6. Asking Sumio about portable stove (Kawamura Main Family House)

Gozo evacuated to Usuda, but in his heart he was thinking, "I would rather work in a munitions factory rather than go to the countryside and suffer one hundred times more. I know I shouldn't say it, but I would rather be in Tokyo with my child than be constrained by the people here." Perhaps he was having problems with some people in Usuda, because he noted in his journal, "This time the quarrel happened because both sides showed their true feelings." Many people who evacuated the cities and had to depend on their country relatives found them closed-minded and had severe conflicts with them. For Gozo, it was particularly hard that they treated him as if he were an American spy.

He took to writing his journal in French and English. This was in part because Gozo was sad about the war, but also because he was feeling nostalgic for his time in France and the United States.

After the war, it wasn't only Gozo and Tsuguharu Foujita who were criticized for having no honor. Many writers, artists, and university professors believed that if people living in Japan did not follow national policy, there would be no way to prevent police from arresting people, torturing them, and coercing them to change their beliefs.

Gozo lived quietly in the countryside of Shinano, trying not to draw attention to himself. Then on August 15, 1945, Japan declared defeat, and the war finally came to an end.

Twelve

Lois Johnson's Reminiscences (October 1998)

Finding a Living Witness

In the state of Maine, at the northernmost point of the Atlantic coast of the United States in a small town called Lubec, lives the only person alive who really knew Gozo. I wanted to meet her so badly that I did everything I could to find her address. While I was at the Great People of Kanazawa Memorial Museum in the City of Kanazawa, I learned that Shiori's third daughter, Junko Sato, was living in Yokosuka City. I thought this was a great stroke of luck.

At the time when the Great People of Kanazawa Memorial Museum was being established, I was coincidentally working on a book called *Takamine Jokichi and His Wife*, and so I helped to gather together some of Takamine's belongings and records that were still in the United States. However, after the Museum of Great People was completed, Takamine's death mask was suddenly discovered, and the surviving family members of the artist who had made it offered to donate the mask to the museum. This offer had come from Junko Sato in Yokosuka. The mask turned out to have been made by Gozo.

I had just begun writing this biography, so as soon as I found out about this, I flew straight to Yokosuka. This is where I obtained materials about Gozo Kawamura and his wife, Shiori, and found out that Shiori's

The Life of a Sculptor: Gozo Kawamura

eldest daughter, Sachiko, was living in Boston. After Gozo's death, his family members received help from many of Gozo's friends and were able to return to the United States, but now only Sachiko was there, and she was living in Boston.

I returned quickly from Japan to the United States and called Sachiko. Then I flew from Los Angeles to Boston, rendezvoused with Sachiko at Boston Airport, and learned from her that Lois Johnson, the most reliable living source of information about Gozo, was still in good health. Sachiko and I immediately set off for Maine. From Boston, we rode a small plane, and one hour later, we landed in Bangor, Maine.

When we arrived in Bangor, we learned that there was no train to Lubec, where we were heading. The bus to Lubec left only once a day, and that bus had already left at 1:00 p.m. that day. As there wasn't a lot to do in the small town of Bangor and we were tired from our long journey, we decided to rest in the hotel until the next day. However, the next morning we didn't want to waste the morning waiting for the 1:00 p.m. bus, so we got into a taxi and headed for Lubec.

As we left Bangor, we crossed the Penobscot River, and from then on we drove through a landscape of forests and lakes. As the rain poured down around us, we took detours around the lake and passed through the occasional swampy puddle, and the car struggled to make its way northeast. Maine is a state known for its lakes and swamps and also its pine trees, and the view, which changed constantly from lakes to coastline to lakes again, perhaps as a leftover from the glacial period, was very beautiful. This area had once been inhabited by about twenty-five thousand Algonquians, but after British explorers arrived in the 1600s, they were pushed into the interior of the state. So today, the highways are not lined with stalls selling Native American pottery and basketry as in Arizona and Oklahoma but are instead punctuated by English-style houses and farmhouses and silos.

We drove for two hours. Just when I thought we must be close to our destination, we entered a town called Whiting, where we drove past a fire station, turned right, and found ourselves looking at the sea. We turned right again, looking for School Street. Lois Johnson's house was the third house on the street.

It was a two-story wooden house painted completely white. On the front porch was an old wooden bench. All around the porch were cosmos and begonia flowers, soaked by the late-autumn rains. We got out of the car and walked up the narrow gravel path that led to the front door, but before we rang the bell, Lois Johnson appeared at the door to welcome us. She wore her graying blond hair in a bob of soft curls, her eyes were framed with large pink glasses, and her cheeks were rosy as she beamed warmly at us.

As soon as we stepped into her house, we saw a staircase leading to the second floor. We passed that and entered into a large living room. On the mantelpiece above the fireplace was a Japanese flower vase, a blue-and-white porcelain plate, an Imari bowl, a teapot, cups, and tea bowls—the room had the appearance of an antique shop. At first it seemed cluttered, but it soon became clear that each object had been positioned very thoughtfully and deliberately.

Lois announced that it was already lunchtime and that we should eat. She disappeared into the kitchen and poured hot water from an old kettle that was sitting on the iron stove into a teapot to make us some green tea.

When I asked how she could find green tea in such a tiny village that wasn't even marked on the map, she explained that she sometimes went to Bangor to do her shopping. To my surprise, she then served us white rice and said, "And here's some miso soup," as she poured the soup into bowls for us. She had gone to great trouble to be hospitable to her two Japanese guests. However, when we sipped our miso soup, we knew right away that it didn't have any *dashi* (bonito stock) in it. Without thinking, we exchanged quick glances, but, not wishing to upset Lois, who had gone to so much trouble for us, we decided to enjoy the soup nonetheless.

Then Lois picked up the black lacquered rice bowls and explained that Gozo had left these bowls behind. I put down my chopsticks and picked up a bowl. The lacquer was chipping off in some places, but I could somehow still feel Gozo's warmth through the bowl after sixty years. Gozo and Shiori had undoubtedly left many things like this to Lois when they returned to Japan.

An Excellent, Japan-Loving Apprentice

Lois had worked in Gozo's studio in New York for ten years (1916–1926). From hints in Lois's story, it seemed that Lois and Gozo had been attracted to each other for some time, but in the end their relationship had apparently not gone beyond that of artist and assistant. Because of this, Lois still had deep respect for Gozo and could clearly provide me with a fair assessment of Gozo's character and work.

After lunch, Lois stood up, went back to the kitchen, and brought a cake out of the oven to serve to us. It was perfectly baked and delicious.

Afterward, I asked Lois the question that was troubling me the most: Why did none of Gozo's works bear his signature?

According to Lois, any work that was done in the name of MacMonnies was always considered MacMonnies's work. Even if his assistants were brilliant or in fact did all of the work, in the United States, no credit like "Assistant Gozo Kawamura" would appear on the pieces.

Above: Lois Johnson in Lubec, 1998 (R)
Below: Gozo and Lois on a visit to Duluth in Minnesota, 1936. At this time, Gozo had been hired as the chief sculptor for the Texas Centennial Exposition, and he was known as the "only Japanese Cowboy." (U)

"But then who could prove that Gozo had a hand in the works?" I asked Lois.

She explained that everyone in the world of sculpture knew that Gozo was working in MacMonnies's studio, so people knew that he had worked on the sculptures.

Again I asked, "But future generations wouldn't know Gozo's name, would they?"

But Lois insisted, "That's not true. Many of Gozo's own works have survived, so his artistic honor will still be preserved."

When I told her that Gozo's name was not well known in Japan, she replied with a voice full of expectation, "It's your job to make sure he becomes better known in Japan."

I explained with a pained expression that I knew this but was worried that it seemed like a very difficult task.

To this she replied emphatically, "I can prove that Gozo used his enlarging machine to create the sculptures *The Sword of Justice* (originally by James Earl Fraser in 1935) at the Supreme Court in Washington, DC, the Princeton University Civil War Memorial statue (1922), the New York City Library *Civic Virtue* statue, and the sculptures on the Washington Square Arch in 1918. I have photographs of the production of these statues that will explain everything."

I told her that I would certainly like to make those photographs public. Although our conversation was a relatively quiet one, it was full of passion.

That evening, she wanted to pick some grasses that grew along the beach and invited us to join her. She told us to dress for the cold and put on long boots. We got into her tiny car, which rattled continuously, but perhaps she was used to the noise, as she didn't look at all bothered by it. After a two-minute drive, we arrived at a small building that turned out to be a US-Canada border inspection point.

There was only one inspector in the building, and when she told him that she had guests from Japan with her, he asked to see our passports or other ID papers. What I had thought was a river in front of us was actually a bay of the Atlantic Ocean, and there was a bridge crossing over it. On the other side of the bridge was the province of New Brunswick in Canada. We were Japanese, but we had become US citizens, so we only had to show the inspector our drivers' licenses. Then we crossed the border.

We drove along a narrow, winding road through a forest and at last arrived at the beach. When we got out of the car and looked around, we saw the surface of the water spreading out in front of us quietly and sleekly, as if it had been covered in oil. There were no ripples, even where the water met the rocks, but this wasn't because the water was stagnant. In the spaces between the rocks, slender leaves that looked like chives were growing. We picked some. Lois was a vegetarian, but tonight she was planning to grill chicken for us and would boil these leaves to go with the chicken.

Soon the sun started to lower in the sky, gradually disappearing down into the western sky. She drove along a shortcut with the idea of reaching the border more quickly, but then she suggested we take a quick look at the summerhouse that belonged to the thirty-second president, Franklin D. Roosevelt, so we made a detour. Lois explained that Roosevelt and his wife used this elegant, two-story, barn-like mansion as their villa in the summertime. We couldn't go inside the house, but we were satisfied to have a view of its beauty from the outside. Across the bay in the evening light, we could make out a lighthouse in the distance.

For dinner, we enjoyed the chicken with the grasses that the three of us had picked and some salad. Before we came, Lois had told us that there were no hotels or motels in this tiny village, so we could stay with her. That night we gave in to her kindness, and she offered us a solid old bed covered with a quilt that Lois said she had made herself.

Slightly damp air seemed to be sneaking inside, but the heat from the stove soon warmed up the whole house. It was only October, but it already had the feeling of winter there. Lois threw another log on the fire and sat with a small bronze sculpture resting on her lap. It was called *Hymn to the Sun*, and Gozo had made it. She let her hands stroke it softly. Lois was at peace with having reached old age. She loved Japanese culture, and the watercolors she had painted of Gozo's hometown Usuda based on his stories of his childhood had become connected to her memories of him.

She was reminiscing about staying with Gozo on a farm in Wisconsin, where they spent many days together studying cattle. Not wanting to interrupt her recollections of these days, we sat there quietly. The long silence continued. The fire burned with bright red flames. Occasionally, Lois quietly poked at the logs in the fire to keep the flames alive.

Lois knew Gozo in the prime of his manhood; Sachiko knew him as her stepfather in his later years. I had never met Gozo Kawamura, but I was spinning their various memories of the artist around in my mind.

Top left: Gozo making the prototype for the statue *The Sword of Justice* at the entrance to the US Supreme Court in Washington, DC, completed 1935 (U)
Top right: Lois, who helped complete the final *Justice* statue using the enlarging machine (U)
Bottom: Statues by Gozo at Washington, DC, Supreme Court

The Life of a Sculptor: Gozo Kawamura

The Enlarging Machine

Among the photographs that remained of Gozo at work, there were several of him using the enlarging machine, but it was hard to tell how the machine was structured or how Gozo used it just from the photographs. When I asked Lois about it, she explained that Megargee could give the best explanation of how the machine worked, but she didn't know whether or not he was still alive.

Indeed, there were letters that Megargee wrote to Gozo and notes that the two artists wrote during production, but I realized that, if he were still alive, Megargee must be a very old man by now, and it would be difficult to track him down.

So Lois drew a diagram of the enlarging machine for me. When you use a three-dimensional enlarging apparatus using geometry, you can start with a five-inch-tall bronze sculpture and enlarge it to six or seven feet in height.

She explained that she always stood next to the original statue and assisted Gozo.

Three-dimensional enlarging machines are devices that enable you to measure the angles, height, and thickness of the original model and work from a distance to create the same shape but several times larger than the original form. In the early 1900s, artists didn't have the technology to create a three-dimensional photograph; instead the operation was done using geometry. Nowadays, we can take a three-dimensional photograph of the original model and make a perfect cast of the original. (In 1923, Isao Morioka invented 3D photosculpture.) According to Lois Johnson's sketch, Gozo's enlarging machine appeared fairly simple, but Lois explained that no one could use it. When Gozo returned to Japan in 1940, he brought the machine with him. However, according to his family, it was still in Yokosuka after Gozo died, and it was eventually thrown away.

While Lois Lignell was a student studying Japanese at Columbia University, she worked as Gozo's assistant. Later she married writer and illustrator Ryerson Johnson. When she met Gozo, Ryerson was teaching her how to use a Japanese brush. He was showing her paintings by Japanese artists and explaining how they used the brush to paint them. She particularly liked the work of Korin Ogata (1658–1716). Later, she copied Korin's style in her watercolor illustrations for the successful children's storybooks *Three Japanese Mice and Their Whiskers* (1934) and *Gozo's Wonderful Kite* (1951). In particular, in *Gozo's Wonderful Kite,* Lois gives expression to some of Gozo's memories of his childhood within the structure of a storybook. In the book, she depicted the village of Usuda based on stories Gozo had told her of his childhood mixed with ideas from her own imagination. She told us many stories of the time when she worked with Gozo as his assistant, and she laughed when she told us about the bronze sculpture of the Jersey cow.

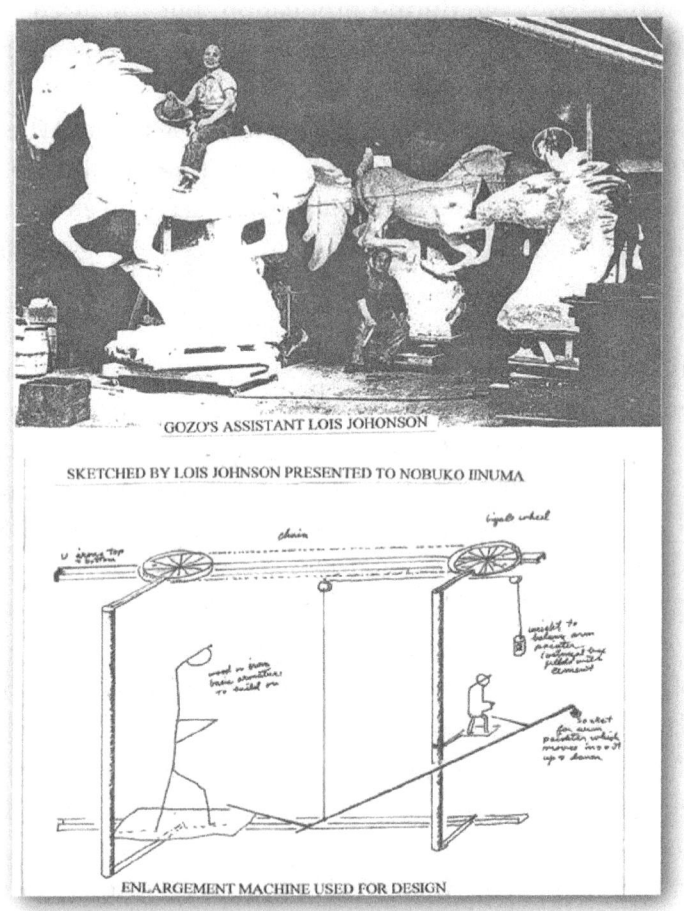

Top: Gozo's assistant, Lois Johnson, on the horse
Bottom: A diagram showing how Gozo's enlarging machine worked, drawn by Lois Johnson (U)

The Life of a Sculptor: Gozo Kawamura

Memories of Gozo and the Cow

While Gozo was living on a dairy farm in Kansas and researching cows, whenever he would go up to the cows, they would apparently run away from him. The image of cows running away from Gozo and the little man running after them became quite a joke. However, when Lois went up to the cows, they would all gather around her and start licking her. It wasn't that the cows had taken a disliking to Gozo as a person. It was that he was so caught up in his research into their form that he touched them too much, and this apparently made them want to keep their distance.

When he was invited to a farm in Minnesota, Pabst, the man who had commissioned Gozo to create the ideal cow, had sent a special train to bring Gozo and his assistant, Lois, from New York to Minnesota. The train was so luxurious that it had its own bathroom suite. Americans certainly treated their artists well!

When Gozo was going through fights with his wife Jeanie, Lois was by his side to offer warm, supportive words. She wasn't encouraging him to divorce her, but Lois was worried that what Jeanie was doing to him would have a detrimental effect on his work.

Lois came to live out in the remote village of Lubec because her uncles had traveled by boat from Massachusetts to Lubec and had built a house with the hope of eventually settling there. However, on one of their trips, the boat sank, killing all of the passengers, leaving the house empty. Lois decided to buy the house.

When Gozo and Shiori were on their honeymoon, they visited Lois and spent some time with her in Lubec. When I thought about their visit, it seemed to me that the old house strangely began to acquire more luster.

Lois had lost her husband, Ryerson, two years earlier. He was ninety-two. Now she lived alone. She painted constantly, and her living-room walls were filled with tens of unframed paintings packed closely together. The week before, a reporter had come from a newspaper in New York to interview her. Looking at her standing in front of her eightieth canvas and painting designs of flowers and a tea set, you wouldn't believe that these charming, youthful pastel-colored paintings were the work of a ninety-year-old woman.

The next day, when it came time to leave, Lois told us we didn't have to take the bus and instead offered to drive us back to Bangor. We accepted her kind offer. On our way back to Bangor, we each ate a whole Maine lobster for lunch, our first moment of simple tourism on that trip.

After our three-hour drive to Bangor, I flew back to Los Angeles via Boston, where I said good-bye to Sachiko. The entire journey from our house in Los Angeles to Bangor and back again was 10,000 km—a very long trip indeed. Sometimes when I have been gathering data, I have been in touch with people only once. However, when I spoke later to Sachiko and Lois on the phone, they both seemed well, and we promised to meet again.

The children's story "Gozo's Wonderful Kite," written by Ryerson Johnson, with illustrations by Lois Lignell (Courtesy of Lois Johnson) (R)

Thirteen

People Associated with Gozo (October 1999)

Greater East Asia Group Sculpture Model Kazuo Hamada

The publisher of this book, Mr. Masao Yoshikawa of Maijisha Publishers, conducted research to discover whether or not Gozo Kawamura's statue *The Greater East Asia Group Sculpture* actually existed at the Yasukuni Shrine. When he visited the shrine to confirm whether the statue was in the Yushukan, one of the shrine's treasure houses, the story he was told there was like a dream.

Mr. Masao Yoshikawa met with the head of the Yasukuni Shrine's Historical Records Department, Takeo Inagami. When he had finished explaining about our biography of Gozo Kawamura, Inagami said, "Now that you mention it, there was an article in a magazine about the man who made that model," and he brought out a copy of the article. In it was a story of a man called Kazuo Hamada, who was the model for the group statue. Mr. Yoshikawa quickly made a call to the magazine's publisher, found the man's contact information, and called him. Then he interviewed him.

The Greater East Asia Group Sculpture: The sculpture depicts a young man representing Japan leading other Asian nations. He stands looking straight ahead holding a sword firmly in one hand. Around him are a child, representing the future of Japan, and a Japanese dog. With his other hand, the young man is helping lift up another young man who appears sickly and probably symbolizes other Asian countries that have been oppressed by the West. Behind him is a young mother holding a child who looks as if he is praying.

The man who posed as a young man as the Japanese savior figure in the statue was still in good health and living in Ichihara City in Chiba Prefecture.

My publisher immediately sent me the details of this story and a copy of the article from the magazine *Kaiko* via fax. *Kaiko* was a magazine put out by graduates of Japan's military academy. Just looking at the photograph of the group sculpture in the magazine sent me back fifty years into my past. When the war began, I was in the third grade of elementary school, and as I looked at the image, the feeling of being at war woke up in me again.

On the way to school, we would sing military-training drill songs, and as a celebration after the fall of Singapore, we marched in a procession, happily shouting, "We won! We won!" Balls made from rubber from the South Pacific were given to elementary-school students all over Japan.

Oh, how the young women yearned for the dashing young men in their Army Academy or Naval Academy uniforms! Even now, I can picture the behavior of my three elder sisters.

In the midst of this wartime atmosphere, Hamada was living in Kyodo in Setagaya in Tokyo while he attended military school. This was the same neighborhood where Gozo lived. Gozo noticed the handsome young Hamada passing by in front of his house, and deciding that no one else but he would do for his model, Gozo approached the landlady of Hamada's lodging house to see if he could hire Hamada as a model.

At that time, Hamada was six feet tall and weighed 165 pounds. He had the dignified appearance of military cadet, a quality I could still see in him now at age seventy-nine.

The Life of a Sculptor: Gozo Kawamura

NOBUKO IINUMA AND KAZUO HAMADA(MAN IN THE STATUE)

STATUE AT YASUKUNI SHRINE ,1942

Top: Kazuo Hamada (right) recounting his memories of his time with Gozo to the author (R)
Bottom: *The Great East Asia Sculpture Group*. The statue can be viewed from all sides. On the reverse is the figure of a mother holding her baby. Completed December 3, 1942 (In the collection of the Yasukuni Shrine) (U)

Hamada went to Gozo's house every day at six in the evening and stayed for about forty minutes. He was always alone with Gozo in the studio. His family members never came in. Hamada put on a loincloth, wrapped a headband around his head, and stood up on the model platform.

Gozo had measured the naked Hamada's hands, arms, and thighs several times, and he touched his back and his shoulders over and over again. This made Hamada feel strange.

Gozo, who had been born in Shinshu and had gone to America and Paris and built large sculptures with his hands, was now examining Hamada's body with his eyes while stroking his skin with his soft hands.

This sculptor, who had become well known in America, was now, for the sake of Japan and East Asia, kneading clay and gradually transforming it into a figure.

To help his model relax a little, Gozo entertained him with interesting stories of his time in the United States and France.

Gozo didn't just look at his model and then make a sculpture. He explained to Hamada that if he didn't touch the real thing, he wouldn't understand how to build the bone structure, musculature, and skin.

Hamada asked, "But, Kawamura-sensei, have you ever touched the naked bodies of the women who were your models?"

Gozo answered, "Yes, of course. Only by doing that can I feel the life in their bodies."

When Hamada replied, "How great that must be!" Gozo explained, "Some women I liked, but others I didn't."

With man-to-man conversations like this, Gozo and Hamada were able to relax together in the studio.

When the work was over each evening and Gozo's wife, Shiori, came into the studio with a bottle of sake and a plate of appetizers, Hamada said he felt both relieved and very happy.

During the war, all necessities for daily life were rationed, and most families could not obtain luxury goods like alcohol and cigarettes, so Hamada, who had heard that these goods were out there somewhere, always looked forward to his evenings working as a model.

Upon completion, the *Greater East Asia Group Sculpture* was presented to the Yasukuni Shrine on December 7, 1942, exactly one year after Japan had entered World War II.

After Japan lost the war, the following episode occurred.

When the Occupying forces visited the Yasukuni Shrine, they thought that the young man in the bronze group with his Japanese sword drawn might incite some people to fight, so they decided to remove the sword and keep it elsewhere. But as soon as they realized that the statue was the work of Gozo, they said there was no problem with it and gave permission for it to remain in the shrine. Since then, the statue has been stored carefully in the shrine's treasure house. However, no matter how hard they looked, the sword was never found.

Once the Occupying forces found out that Gozo was alive and well, they started the chain of events that began with his being hired as an interpreter in Nagano Prefecture. In particular, General Eichelberger had known of Gozo's work and talent back in the United States, and hoping that Gozo's knowledge of both Japanese and American cultures could help ensure the success of the American Occupation of Japan, he requested that Gozo be hired not only as an interpreter but as more of an adviser.

At this point there are, no doubt, some people who would question Gozo's integrity. But I certainly don't. I propose that Gozo acted as a cultural bridge across the Pacific, connecting Japan and the United States.

As Gozo Kawamura's biographer, I am more than delighted that his *Great East Asia Group Sculpture* was rediscovered after fifty years. What was previously known only to the young soldier Kazuo Hamada can now be brought out into the light for art lovers to see and appreciate.

Masaji Watanabe, Gozo's Hospital Roommate

On June 8, 1999, my essay entitled "Japan's Forgotten Maestro of Sculpture" was published in the culture section of the *Nihon Keizai Shinbun* (the *Japan Economic Times*).

Then a few days later, I received a phone call at home from Hiroyuki Kohashi, the assistant chief of the Culture section of the *Nihon Keizai*

Shinbun. He told me that they had heard from someone who said that they had known Gozo, and he thought that it might be useful for my research if I talked directly with this person.

Masaji Watanabe recalling his memories of Gozo's last days in the hospital room they shared (R)

I checked my schedule for my next trip to Japan and got in touch with him right away. It was more good news.

The person was a seventy-year-old man named Masaji Watanabe who lived in Fujisawa City in Kanagawa Prefecture. I made an appointment to meet with him in the fall, on October 23.

Mr. Watanabe had been hospitalized for tuberculosis of the kidneys from June to August 1949 at St. Joseph's Hospital (formerly the Japanese Military Hospital) in Yokosuka. While in the hospital, he had become friendly with an older patient in a bed diagonally opposite, who

The Life of a Sculptor: Gozo Kawamura

turned out to be a talkative sculptor called Gozo Kawamura. In that large room, Watanabe, another man who had just graduated from the Naval Academy, and a third young man would go over to Gozo and listen to his stories of France.

"Tsuguharu Foujita was a bit odd, you know. I wasn't that close to him really," he would say jokingly.

Gozo Kawamura was apparently already in the final stages of his stomach cancer. Almost every day, he would receive visits from American soldiers. In particular, Naval Lieutenant General Decker visited him on many occasions. Decker brought him milk and chocolates, but Gozo didn't eat any of them; instead he gave them to Watanabe and the other young men.

"Even though everyone is nice to me, I still get angry sometimes. It's not good for your health to suppress your feelings," Gozo would often say.

His symptoms were progressing quickly. Eventually the doctors operated on his stomach. At the time of the surgery, Gozo was drained of his physical and mental strength. Whenever he saw Watanabe, he said, "When it comes to this, all you can do is entrust yourself to the gods."

Soon, Watanabe was able to return home. Gozo had clearly become fond of the young man, and after he left, Gozo sent him a postcard written in tiny letters. Unfortunately, Watanabe no longer had the postcard, but he continued to share his memories of Gozo with me.

In the hospital, Gozo wore fashionable pajamas and a silk gown—you could tell he had lived abroad.

He may have been small, but he was indeed a classy man. And, Watanabe remembered, he would often walk around the hospital room holding a cane.

Gozo told the young men, "America and Japan shouldn't have gone to war. The Japanese just don't know the Americans. It was such a shame." He wanted them to understand his point of view as someone who had experienced life in other countries.

Whenever Watanabe and the other young men visited with Gozo in the hospital room, they had had meaningful conversations. Of all the things Gozo said, the following words had left the strongest impression on Watanabe:

"In a man's life there are plenty of opportunities to make money dishonestly. You have to resist those chances."

Watanabe had always kept those words in his heart as a moral compass.

Gozo had also advised them to be very careful with women, particularly when the marriage was on the rocks. He warned them that even if you can see your wife's flaws, you should wait until the divorce is official before you start seeing another woman. A man can be landed with a completely unreasonable divorce settlement, and it can hurt him for the rest of his life.

Perhaps this was what Gozo was feeling about himself.

He told through his experiences of marriage, full of unhappiness with his first wife, Jeanie.

For Masaji Watanabe, being able to tell his stories about Gozo Kawamura must have made him feel nostalgic about his own youth.

The day before (October 22, 1999), I had met with Kazuo Hamada, and that day, I was meeting with Masaji Watanabe. Now, after meeting these two people who were connected to Gozo, my final research in Japan was complete. The deep, blue autumn sky seemed exceptionally beautiful that day.

Fourteen

Gozo Kawamura Materials

Gozo Kawamura Museum Pictures/Gozo's Home Pictures

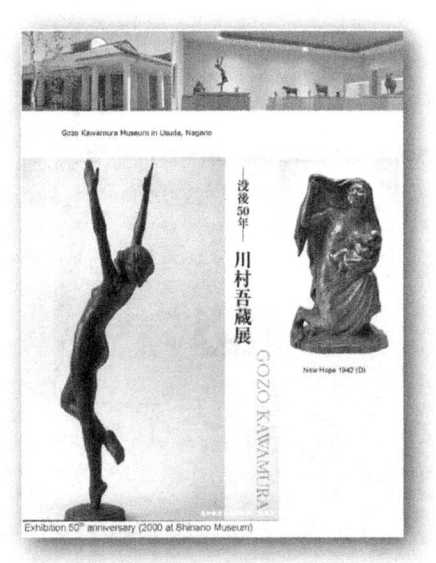

Top: Gozo Kawamura Museum in Usuda, Nagano (Google)
Bottom left: Catalog of Gozo Kawamura Exhibition (Fiftieth anniversary of Gozo's death) at Shinano Museum in Nagano
Bottom right: Bronze New Hope 1942 (D)

Nobuko Iinuma

House of Gozo Kawamura, Usuda Nagano

Gozo Kawamura memorial museum in Saku, Nagano

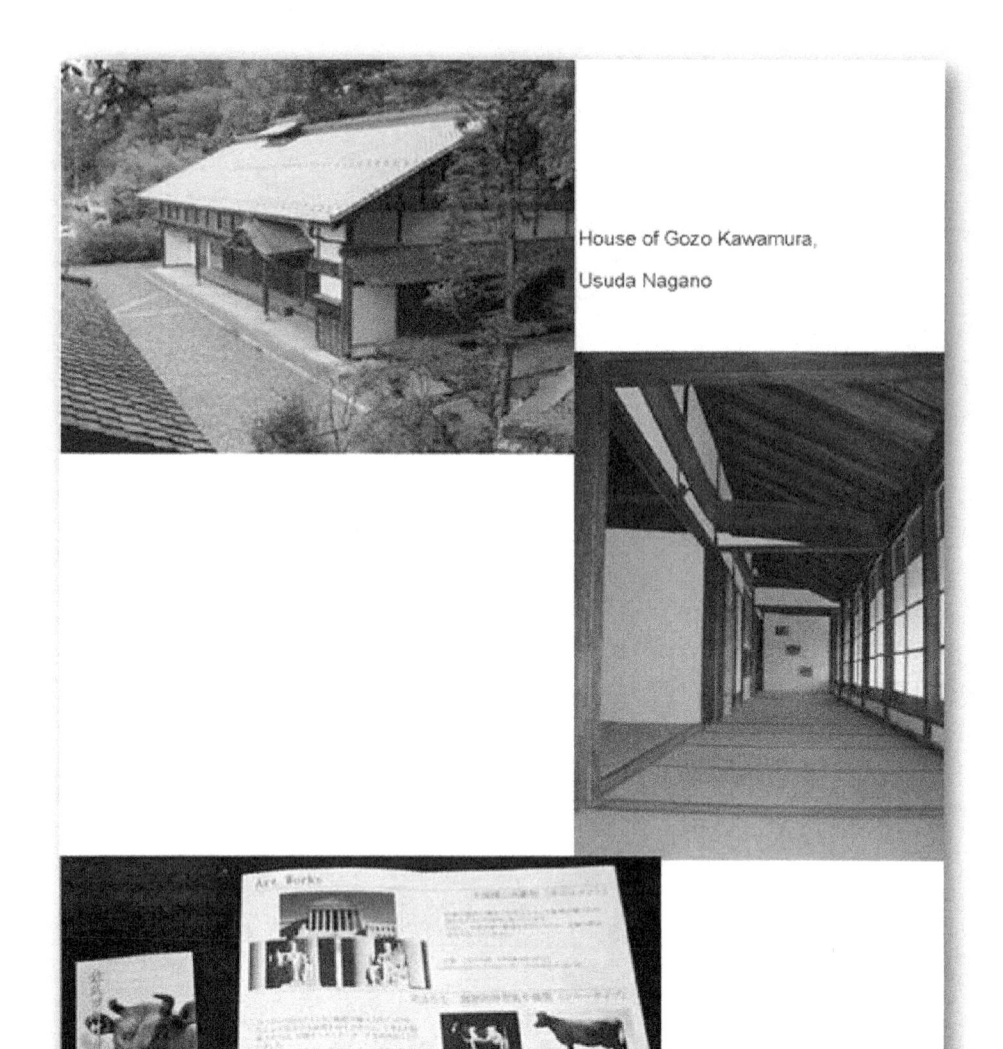

Top left and right: Home of Gozo Kawamura, Usuda Nagano
Bottom: Gozo Kawamura Memorial Museum in Saku, Nagano

The Life of a Sculptor: Gozo Kawamura

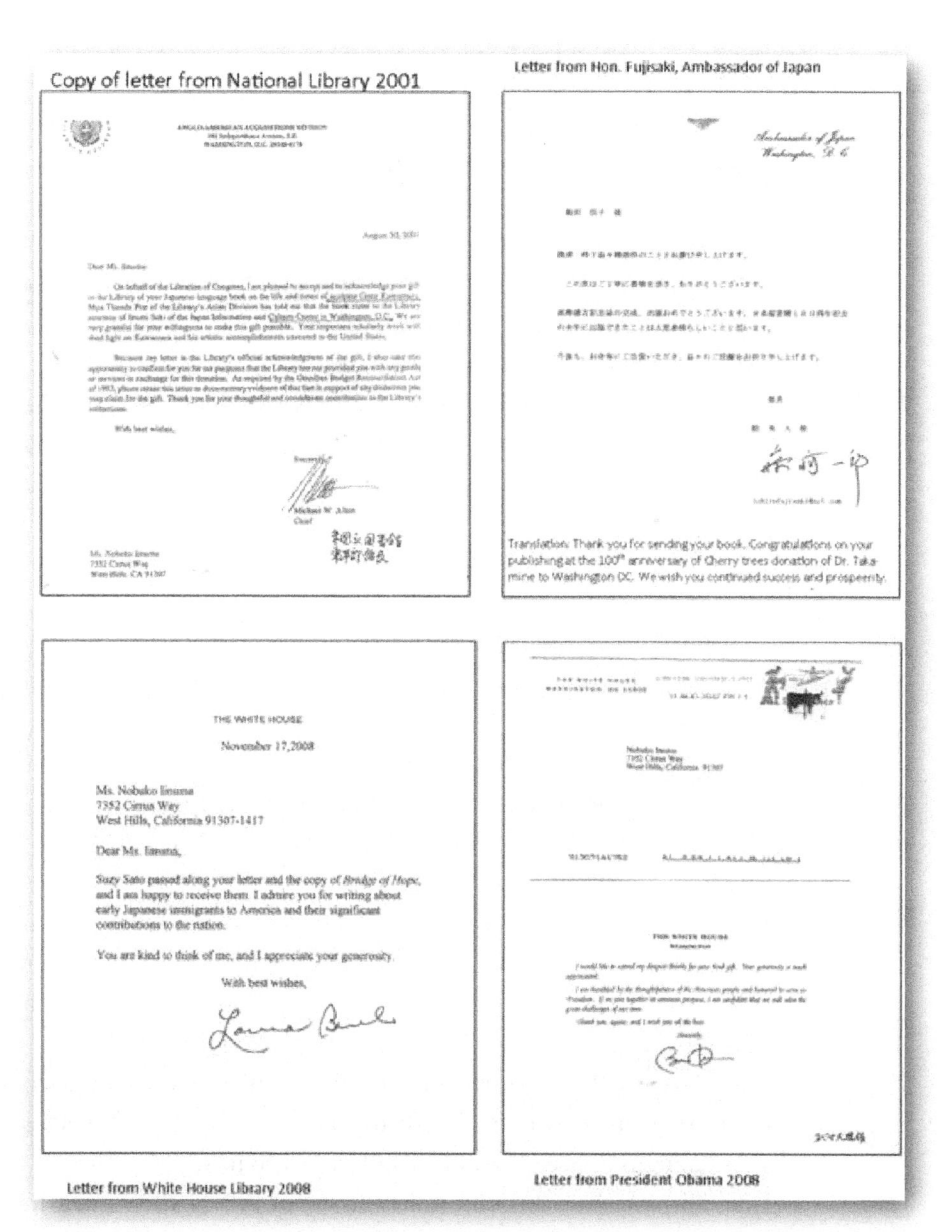

Top left: Appreciation letter from National Library in DC, 2001
Top right: Appreciation letter from Hon. Ichiro Fujisaki, ambassador of Japan
(Translation is below) 2008
Bottom left: Appreciation letter from White House Library, 2008
Bottom right: Appreciation letter from President Obama, 2008

Gozo Kawamura Chronology
(Note: Gozo's age is given in parenthesis in the year column)

1884	August 17: Gozo Kawamura, the third son to Kawamura Heijiro and Semu, is born at house #173, Usuda Village, South Saku District, Nagano Prefecture.
1888	>December: Construction of the National Railroad's Naoetsu Line between Karuizawa and Ueda.
1891	Gozo enters Usuda Elementary School.
1893	>Usuda Mura receives town status and becomes Usuda Cho.
1897	April: Gozo enters Nagano Middle School Ueda Branch (which later became the Nagano Prefectural School Ueda Middle School).
1900	>October: Gozo's relative Banka Maruyama travels to the United States.
1901	>September: Banka Maruyama returns to Japan.
1902	Around this time, Gozo is influenced by Banka Maruyama and another relative, Kiyoko Yamamoto, to dream of traveling to the United States.
1903 (19)	March: Gozo graduates from Ueda Middle School. May 22: Gozo's father, Heijiro, dies at age sixty-five. July 24: Gozo's mother, Semu, dies at age fifty-seven. Around this time, Gozo is invited by Mayor Akaoka Seikichi of Kirihara Village, South Saku, where his elder brother's wife came from, to work as a substitute teacher at Kirihara Elementary School.
1904	May: On the first anniversary of their father's death, Gozo tells his brothers of his desire to become an artist. Receives their permission to travel to the United States.
(20)	July 25: Just after the first anniversary of his mother's death, Gozo leaves Usuda. August 3: Gozo sets sail from Yokohama to San Francisco. Then travels to New York, then Boston.

	In Boston, visits Bunkyo Matsuki (his guarantor) and works in his art shop, while taking classes in English at a Boston high school.
	Enrolls in Queens Design School. Becomes an assistant to Henry Hudson Kitson, a sculptor at the school, and learns the basics of sculpture.
1906 (22)	September: Moves into Kitson's house (until October 1907). December: Visits New York, interviews with Professor R. T. Bain at the National Academy of Design, and promises to become her assistant.
1907 (23)	June: Enters New York's National Academy of Design. >The National Academy was established by Samuel Morse, who also invented the Morse code. Gozo moves into Professor Bain's studio and improves the function of her sculptural enlarging machine (which was to be a great resource to Gozo later).
1908 (24)	Wins first prize in the academy's sculpture competition and receives thirty dollars in prize money.
1909 (25)	Graduates from the National Academy of Design. Gozo decides he wants to travel to France to study. As next step, Professor Bain writes a recommendation letter to Frederick W. MacMonnies, an American sculptor working in Paris, on Gozo's behalf.
1910	July: Gozo travels to France, becomes MacMonnies's assistant, and moves into his home. Soon afterward, while working as his assistant, he visits the Louvre regularly and sketches artworks in the galleries.
1911	Travels with MacMonnies and his wife to Italy, Britain, and other parts of Europe.
1912	Passes the entrance exam for the École des Beaux-Arts and begins his studies there.

(28)	Around this time is asked by Rodin to become his assistant but turns him down.
	>July 30: In Japan, the Taisho Era (1912–1926) begins.
1913	Becomes a scholarship student in the École des Beaux-Arts Sculpture Department.
(29)	MacMonnies receives a commission from the mayor of New York City to build a sculptural monument. MacMonnies begins work on the small-scale model for the monument.
1914	>August 14: World War I begins.
(30)	Meets Toson Shimazaki in Paris. Helps find him a hiding place in Limoges in the South of France.
	Production at MacMonnies's studio is halted briefly. MacMonnies's house and studio in Giverny are converted into a hospital for injured soldiers and used by the Red Cross. Gozo evacuates with MacMonnies and his wife to England briefly.
1915	Returns to Paris. Helps MacMonnies build the small-scale models for the sculptural commissions *Civic Virtue* and the George Washington War Memorial.
1916	Around this time, Gozo begins working with the enlarging machine he designed to enlarge MacMonnies's statues.
(32)	August 12: marries Jeanie Farque.
	Around this time, Gozo receives a letter from Fred Pabst and the American Jersey Cow Association asking him to design a sculpture of the ideal cow.
1917	Submits work to the National Academy in New York: *Hymn to the Sun*, *Defense*, and bust sculptures of Thomas Hastings and Granville Smith.
(33)	>November 17: Rodin dies.
1918	>November 30: World War I ends.
	Turns thirty-four. Completes sculptures with MacMonnies on Washington Square Arch in New York City.
1921	Becomes friends with Hideyo Noguchi.

1922	Completes with MacMonnies the fountain sculpture *Civic Virtue* in front of New York City Hall.
(38)	Completes with MacMonnies the two sculptures, *Beauty* and *Philosophy*, flanking the entrance to the New York Municipal Library.
June: Completes with MacMonnies the George Washington statue for Civil War Memorial on the grounds of Princeton University.
July 23: Jokichi Takamine dies in New York. Gozo makes a death mask.
October: Establishes the *Gachokai*, or Painters and Sculptors Club, with fourteen Japanese artists living in New York, including Eitaro Ishigaki and Yasuo Kuniyoshi.
November: Submits six works, including *Master James, Holstein Bull,* and *Holstein Cow: Female,* to the Painting and Sculpture Exhibition of the New York Japanese Artists Association (the first exhibition of the *Gachokai?*).
1923:	Completes his sculptures of his ideal cows, *Jersey Dairy Bull* and *Jersey Dairy Cow (female)*, and receives high praise in newspapers and magazines.
(39)	Receives order for a bust sculpture from Kentaro Kataoka, president of Kataoka Silk Company, while on his research trip to Europe and the United States.
>August: President Calvin Coolidge takes office.
>September 1: The Great Kanto Earthquake in Japan.
Gozo receives a commission to create a bust sculpture of President Coolidge.
1924	>New immigration laws pass in the United States. Japanese immigrants are completely prohibited.
Gozo completes busts of President Coolidge's, his mentor MacMonnies, and the late Prince Hirotada Kacho
1925	Completes statue called *Pocket Monkey*.
1926	>Showa era begins in Japan (1926–1989).

Nobuko Iinuma

1927	February: Submits four works, including *Spring*, to the exhibition of Japanese artists' work organized by the New York Shimposha Shusai Hojin. May: Completes sculpture portrait of Adam Wigners.
1928	>May 21: Hideyo Noguchi dies in Accra, Africa, while on a research trip there.
(44)	From this year, works on sculptures *President Andrew Jackson on Horseback*, *General Lee on Horseback*, *George Washington on Horseback*, and *Theodore Roosevelt on Horseback*. Makes two hundred sculptures of his Holstein cow and sends them to agricultural schools and farms all over the United States.
1930	May: Sculpture of Kanetaro Katakura is taken back to Japan by Katakura's brother Gosuke Imai. Creates *Young Man Raising an Arm*, *Peter Pan*, and *Blue River*.
1931	Creates *Reflecting Water*.
1934	Creates *Torso*.
1935	July 10: Divorce settlement with ex-wife, Jeanie, finalized (final payment of divorce settlement).
(51)	Completes with James E. Fraser (one of MacMonnies's pupils) the pair of statues *Justice* at the entrance to the US Supreme Court in Washington, DC.
1936	September: Takes photographs of Toson Shimazaki while he was in the United States in preparation to make his bust sculpture. Creates a large group of sculptures as the chief sculptor for the Centennial of the State of Texas Exhibition.
1937	>April 15: Helen Keller visits Japan for the first time.
(53)	Bust of Mr. Proctor. >Receives gift of painting *Young Woman* from Kyohei Inukai. >MacMonnies dies at age seventy-four. >October 14: Shiori Maeno (whom Gozo later marries) comes to the United States as part of Waka Yamada's Women's US Research Group. Around this time, Gozo becomes ill and while hospitalized meets Shiori Maeno, who was introduced to him by Tamotsu

The Life of a Sculptor: Gozo Kawamura

	Minowa, the New York branch chief of the Yokohama Shokin Ginko (Yokohama Specie Bank Ltd.), originally from Nozawa in South Saku District, Nagano.
1938	Gozo is invited by the American Sculpture Union to give a lecture as part of the Great International Exposition in New York.
1939	>February 26: Japanese Ambassador to the United States Hiroshi Saito dies while in the United States.
	Around this time, it is suggested that Gozo return to Japan.
	March 30: Gozo marries Shiori Maeno.
	April: New York International Exposition opens. Gozo creates sculptures of celestial dancers for the entrance to the Japanese pavilion.
	Creates bust sculptures of Professor Hideyo Noguchi, Ambassador Hiroshi Saito, Dr. Toyohiko Takami, and Lady Geraldine Livingston and creates *Three Female Calves*.
1940	April: Kensuke Horinouchi, the new Japanese ambassador to the United States, and Consul General Kaname Wakasugi in New York both recommend Gozo return to Japan. He decides to return.
	August: Sends two boxes of his sculptures ahead to Japan. Turns fifty-six.
	> October 10: Exhibition celebrating the 2600th Anniversary of the Japanese Imperial System opens.
	>Japan-US relations take a turn for the worse.
	November 10: Gozo and Shiori arrive at Yokohama. Gozo is back in Japan for the first time in thirty-six years.
	December: Gozo rents a house in Kyodo in the Setagaya, Tokyo, and sets up a studio.
1941	Around this time, Gozo pays a visit to all the Imperial families, Toson Shimazaki, Tsuguharu Foujita, Fumio Asakura, and Sesshu Hayakawa.

(53) February: With Ryusaku Tsunoda's letter of introduction, Gozo visits Soho Tokutomi.
Creates statue *Ancient Warrior* for Naval Memorial Day on May 27 and bust sculpture of His Highness Fushimi-no-miya Hiroyoshi.
August: Completes bust statue of Soho Tokutomi, who declares his skills to be "superhuman."
>December 8: Start of War in the Pacific between Japan and the United States.

>Japanese Americans forced into detention centers.

1942 >March 4: Banka Maruyama dies at age seventy-six.
March: Creates bust sculptures of Soho Tokutomi and his wife, commissioned as a presentation gift from the Japanese Newspaper Association.
June: Launch of the Gozo Kawamura Support Association.
Creates statue of Member of the House of Lords Yoshiharu Tadokoro and *New Hope*.
December 7: Gozo's statue *The Great East Asia Sculpture Group* presented to the Yasukuni Shrine.

1943 The Gozo Kawamura Support Association is dissolved and reformed as the Kawamurakai (Kawamura Club).

(59) >August 22, Toson Shimazaki dies at age seventy-one.
October: Gozo completes his sculpture of Toson Shimazaki.

1944 Gozo and family evacuate Tokyo and move to his hometown of Usuda in Nagano Prefecture. Works briefly as a farmer.
Completes sculpture of Old Risuke Uehara and *Morning Prayer*.

1945 >August: US planes bomb areas of Nagano Prefecture.
>August 15: The Pacific War ends.
>August 30: Lieutenant General Eichelberger of the 8th Division of the occupying US Army and General MacArthur, US supreme commander in the Far East, land at Atsuki Airbase. November: US Occupying Forces arrive

The Life of a Sculptor: Gozo Kawamura

	in Karuizawa and commandeer hotels, villas, and golf courses.
	Around this time, Gozo receives an order from GHQ and interviews with Lieutenant General Eichelberger.
1946	January 30: Ordered by the Nagano prefectural government to work as a translator and interpreter. Moves to Karuizawa.
(62)	March: Submits his bust sculpture *Mr. Proctor* (made in 1937) in the first Nitten Exhibition (Japanese national art exhibition).
	Around this time, Gozo begins working on a sculpture of Lieutenant General Eichelberger.
1947	September: Invited by Naval Lieutenant General Decker to serve as principal art advisor for the US forces at the Yokosuka base. Moves to Yokosuka and sets up his studio and home on the third floor of what was originally the Japanese naval officers' assembly room (the Enlisted Men's or EM Club).
(63)	After this, he begins making sculptures of US military officers.
1948	>August 4: Lieutenant General Eichelberger returns to the United States.
(64)	The City of Yokohama commissions him to make a bust statue of Lieutenant General Eichelberger.
	December: Finishes work on *Easter Angel* statue (begun in September). The statue was opened to the public in front of the US naval base in Yokosuka. Creates sculptures of Naval Lieutenant General Griffin, Mrs. Buyers, and Major General McConnell.
1949	The people of Yokosuka commission him to make a bust statue of Naval Lieutenant General Decker and his wife.
(65)	November: Unveiling ceremony for the statue for Naval Lieutenant General and Mrs. Decker. Gozo receives an award of appreciation from the Yokosuka Chamber of Commerce.
	Around this time, his physical condition starts to deteriorate. Begins work on a statue of General MacArthur, commissioned by Kanagawa Prefecture.
	Creates statues of US Ambassador Peter Grimm, Arthur MacArthur (General MacArthur's son), and *Freemason*.

	Is diagnosed with stomach cancer, so has surgery. But later relapses.
1950	March 11: Gozo dies at St. Joseph's Hospital in Yokosuka at the age of sixty-six.
	March 13: Funeral held for him at the Japanese Christian Church Hall in Yokosuka.
	His wife, Shiori, and adopted daughter Sachiko work to complete in bronze Gozo's unfinished sculptures of General MacArthur, Yukio Ozaki (a.k.a. Gakudo Ozaki), and Helen Keller.
	June 17–23: Exhibition of Gozo Kawamura's sculpture opens at the Nihonbashi Mitsukoshi department store, sponsored by the Mainichi Newspaper and Mainichi English Language Newspaper.
	>June 25: Start of the Korean War.
	October: Gozo's bust sculpture of General MacArthur is entered in the sixth Nitten art exhibition and wins in the sculpture category.
	November 28: The unveiling ceremony for Gozo's statue of General MacArthur at the Nihonbashi Mitsukoshi Department Store.
1951	January 26: Kanagawa Prefecture presents the statue of General MacArthur without a cap to the general as a gift for his seventy-first birthday.
	April 22: General MacArthur retires as supreme commander of the Allied forces.

Chronology Notes: All ages are given in the Japanese manner, namely adding another year every January first. This chronology was compiled using a chronology of Gozo Kawamura's life from 1942, Gozo's own journal and notes, materials from the Shinano Museum in Nagano, and from later investigations by the author.

The Life of a Sculptor: Gozo Kawamura

List of Works by Gozo Kawamura

Name	Year/Gozo's age	Size (cm, unless otherwise stated)	Material	Notes/page mentioned in book
Edwin Booth Memorial	1913 (age 29)	Unknown	?	Made with MacMonnies?
Bust of Margaret Draper		Details unknown	?	Made with MacMonnies?
Standing Figure of Edith Good		Details unknown	?	Made with MacMonnies?
Hymn to the Sun	1917 (age 33)	55x12x18	bronze	
Defense (?)		34x29x18	bronze	
Bust of Thomas Hasting (?)		Details unknown		
Bust of Granville Smith		Details unknown		
Peace Arch/War Memorial (Washington Square, NYC)	1918 (age 34)	12mx8m	marble	Monumental sculpture collaboration with MacMonnies
Civic Virtue (fountain sculpture in garden in front of NY City Hall)	1922 (age 38)	6m (base 8m)	marble (22 tons approx.)	Monumental sculpture collaboration with MacMonnies
Beauty and Philosophy (Figures flanking entrance to NY Municipal Library)	1922	7mx4m	marble	Monumental sculpture collaboration with MacMonnies
George Washington Battle Monument (Princeton University)	1922	12mx8m	marble (40 tons approx.)	Monumental sculpture collaboration with MacMonnies
Master James	1922	Details unknown		
Jersey Dairy Cow (male)	1923	46x63x23	bronze	
Holstein Dairy Cow (male)	age 39	48x72x24	bronze	
Holstein Dairy Cow (female)	age 39	46x64x23	bronze	
Bust of President Calvin Coolidge	1924	73x60x36	plaster	Needs repair
Bust of Frederick MacMonnies	age 40	63x50x32	painted plaster	
The Late Prince His Highness Kachonomiya Hirotada-O	age 40	Details unknown		
Pocket Monkey	1925	21x19x15	bronze	
Adam Wigners (?)	1927	Details unknown		A monument?
Andrew Jackson on Horseback	1928 – after	Details unknown		A monument?
General Lee on Horseback	1928 – after	Details unknown		A monument?
George Washington on Horseback	1928 – after	Details unknown		A monument?
Theodore Roosevelt on Horseback	1928 – after	Details unknown		A monument?
Bust of Kentaro Katakura	1930	60x34x31	white marble	In the Katakurakan Museum
Young Man Raising his Arm	age 46	52x15x20	bronze	
Peter Pan	age 46	39x22x16	bronze	
Blue River	age 46	32x28x9	bronze	
Reflecting Water	1931	42x29x16	painted plaster	Damaged, needs repair
Torso	1934	75x26x22	bronze	
Justice (Pair of Sculptures flanking entrance to the U.S. Supreme Court, Washington D.C.)	1935	3mx2m each	marble	Monumental sculpture collaboration with Fraser
Spring	1937	10x39x14	bronze	

Title	Date/Age	Dimensions	Material	Notes
Bust of Mr. Proctor	1937	48x21x24	bronze	
Celestial Dancers For the Japanese Pavilion entrance at the NYC International	1939 / age 55	6mx8m	?	Monumental sculpture commissioned by the Japanese government
Bust of Dr. Hideo Noguchi	1939	60x34x26	bronze	
Bust of Ambassador Hiroshi Saito	age 55	76x47x30	bronze	
Sitting Calf	age 55	13x24x13	bronze	
Standing Calf	age 55	24x28x10	bronze	
Calf Eating Grass	age 55	22x25x10	bronze	
Dr. Toyohiko Takami	age 55	Details unknown		Only seen in a photo
Geraldine Livingston	age 55	Details unknown		Only seen in a photo
Amazon	1940	49x32x21	bronze	
Bust of Soho Tokutomi (Japanese dress)	1941	74x63x37	bronze	In the Soho Tokutomi Memorial Museum
Ancient Warrior	age 57	Details unknown		Only seen in a photo
Bust of His Highness Fushiminomiya Hiroyoshi	age 57	Details unknown		
Bust of Member of the House of Lords Yoshiharu Tadokoro	1942	Details unknown		Only seen in a photo
Bust of Soho Tokutomi (Western dress)	age 58	72x47x33	painted plaster	In the Ochanomizu Library Storage
Bust of Soho Tokutomi's wife	age 58	65x44x30	Painted plaster	In the Ochanomizu Library Storage
New Hope	age 58	35x22x19	bronze	
The Great East Asia Sculpture Group	age 58	59x38x38	bronze	In the Yasukuni Shrine Storage
Bust of Toson Shimazaki	1943	46x30x24	bronze	
Bust of Old Rosuke Uehara	1944	38x29x25	bronze	Kawamura Family Storage (relatives)
Morning Prayer	1944	21x31x13	painted plaster	
Bust of Lieutenant General Eichelberger	1948	51x30x25	bronze	
Bust of Major General McConnell	age 64	Details unknown		Only seen in a photo
Bust of Naval Lieutenant General Griffin	age 64	49x25x26	bronze	
Bust of Mrs. Buyers, wife of Major	Age 64	37x21x12	painted plaster	
Bust of Naval Lieutenant General Decker	1949	51x26x25	bronze	
Bust of Naval Lieutenant General Decker's wife	age 65	51x28x24	bronze	
Bust of General MacArthur	1949	81x62x32	painted plaster	
Bust of Arthur MacArthur	1949	21x14x11	bronze	
Bust of John Moor Allison, later US Ambassador to Japan (?)	1949	54x32x26	painted plaster	
Bust of Mr. Peter Grimm	1949	57x35x25	painted plaster	
Freemason	1949	Details unknown		Only seen in a photo
Bust of theology professor Dr. Daniel	1950	55x35x26	painted plaster	
Bust of Helen Keller	age 66	53x28x26	bronze	
Bust of Yukio Ozaki	age 66	66x48x31	painted plaster	Needs repair

Notes: This table was created using materials from the Shinano Museum in Nagano. For all works outside Nagano Prefecture, the data was compiled from notes taken during the author's investigations.

However, the sizes of the monumental sculptures in the United States are only estimates made by the author when visiting the sites. Among those works that have no noted description of location are works belonging to Nagano Usuda Cultural Center.

Key to Photography Credits
U: City of Saku, Usuda Cultural Center. Photography courtesy of Sue Kawamura
D: Daiichi Seimei. Photography by Kazuyuki Yazawa
Y: Kazuyuki Yazawa
R: Photography by the author
E: Photography by the editor/publisher

Reference Materials

(Japanese-language sources)
"Gozo Kawamura Chronology." *Gozo Kawamura Support Association Prospectus* (June 1942).

Kawamura, Shiori (pub.). "Gozo Kawamura Chronology." Guidebook. (1978).

Kawamura, Gozo. Notebooks/journals.

Kawamura, Yoichiro. "Sculptor Gozo Kawamura: His Works and Life." Private publication, March 28, 1990.

Daiichi Seimei (pub.). *Traditional Sculpture: GOZO.* Exhibition Catalog (November 1995).

Japanese American Artists Living in the United States. Exhibition Catalog (Tokyo Metropolitan Teien Art Museum, August 1995).

Geijutsu Shincho (*New Tides in Art*, Japanese art magazine) October (1995).

Geijutsu Shincho (*New Tides in Art*, Japanese art magazine) January (1996).

Dictionary of Japanese Modern Art History (Kodansha).

Japanese Art Almanac, 1947–1951. Art Research Center.

Mainichi Shinbun Newspaper:
March 17, 1950 (evening edition)
March 31, 1950 (evening edition)
June 19, 1950 (evening edition)

September 2, 1950 (Kanagawa edition)
October 29, 1950 (Kanagawa edition)
November 26, 1950 (daily)
November 29, 1950 (daily)
March 13, 1951 (Nagano edition)
August 17, 1983 (Nagano edition)
Asahi Shinbun **Newspaper:**
February 9, 1941 (daily)
December 24, 1948 (daily)
November 28, 1950 (evening edition)
August 15, 1983 (Nagano edition)
Yomiuri Shinbun **Newspaper**
November 5, 1950 (daily)
March 9, 1978 (Nagano edition)
August 15, 1983 (Nagano edition)
May 3, 1994 (Nagano edition)
July 15, 1995 (Kanazawa edition)

(English-language sources)
New York Times: June 23, 1922/ December 31, 1939
Canada New Paper: June 6, 1922
Cleveland Paper: June 5, 1923
Duluth Herald: August 1936
The Holstein Breeder and Dairyman June 8, 1922
Nippon Times: June 1949/November 1950/January 1951
Japan Times and Mail (name later changed to *Japan Times*): February 10, 1926

Acknowledgments

The following people provided much assistance and support for this book:

The staff of the Reference Room, at City of Saku, Usuda Cultural Center inNagano Prefecture
- Former Director of the Culture Center, Masatoshi Maruyama
- First Director of the Culture Center, Sakuo Kitahara
- Yoichiro Kawamura for materials
- Sue Kawamura and Nobuko Kawamura
- Lois Johnson, Artist
- Nagae Teruyo, Director of the Kyoka Izumi Translation Office
- Sachiko Pluart
- Junko Sato
- Hiroko Maki
- Takeo Kaji, Photojournalist
- Jiro Ueda, Smithsonian Institution, Freer Gallery, Conservation Department.
- Masayuki Okabe, Assistant Professor in the Literature and History Departments of Teikyo University
- Dr. Herbert Plutchow, Professor, California State University, Los Angeles
- Junko Shiba, Japanese-French Simultaneous Translator
- Akiko Miyazaki
- Takeo Inagami, Yasukuni Shrine Historical Records Department
- Hiromichi Kimura, Emeritus Professor, Kanazawa Bijutsu Kogei Daigaku (Kanazawa Art and Craft University)
- Oki Sachiko, Assistant, Kanazawa Bijutsu Kogei Daigaku
- Nanen Kitamura, Calligrapher and Seal Carver
- Nagano Shinano Art Museum
- Fuchu Art Museum
- Kazuo Hamada
- Masaji Watanabe

Afterword

Most tourists who visit New York undoubtedly go sightseeing in Greenwich Village and Washington Square. In Washington Square there is an arch that looks like the Arc de Triomphe in Paris, but none of the Japanese tourists looking up at the arch would imagine a Japanese sculptor had worked on its statues.

Many visitors to Washington, DC, know that the rows of cherry trees that line the Potomac River were given by Japan to the United States in 1911 to commemorate the friendship between Washington and Tokyo. But very few people know that the Japanese chemist Jokichi Takamine helped make that gift happen. Many people think that the achievement belonged to Yukio Ozaki alone.

Was Gozo, who was discovered by MacMonnies and hired as his assistant, happy in the end with his achievements as an artist? With MacMonnies, Gozo had to work behind the scenes, far from the spotlight, for half of his life. Since Gozo's career as an individual artist only really took off after MacMonnies died, it isn't too much to say that MacMonnies took advantage of Gozo's talents to profit himself as an artist. While Gozo saw all of his experiences as part of his training, there must have been times when he was frustrated with an apprenticeship system that didn't allow him to bask in the light of success too. MacMonnies didn't have any children, and he loved Gozo like his own child, but this wasn't the only reason he kept Gozo in the shadows. It is very likely that MacMonnies didn't want to share Gozo and his talents with anyone else. It was only when Gozo started to make his bronze cows that he was at last able to enjoy the spotlight.

Gozo returned to Japan in 1940. Because of the war and his own illness, he departed this world before the Japanese people could know of his success as an artist in the United States. "Save Gozo!" The headline in the *Mainichi Shinbun* newspaper on March 17, 1950, was not a cry for help to save him from illness. It was an appeal to the people of Japan not to let him disappear or be forgotten. Sadly, on March 11, Gozo had passed away. The cry was in vain, and his light went out.

Before he died, he had demanded of his wife, Shiori, "Take a photograph of me like this." He made her take a picture of his naked skinny body. To the end, Gozo maintained his artistic curiosity, studying his physical form as his life was passing from him.

As a young man at the École des Beaux-Arts, he had loved studying anatomy, and in order to create his perfect cow, he had avidly researched zoology, anatomy, and physiology. This request to Shiori was so like Gozo.

In November 1995, to mark fifty years since the end of World War II, an exhibition of Gozo Kawamura's work was held at the Daiichi Seimei Hall in Marunouchi, Tokyo. For me, this was a very happy occasion.

Miraculously, the location of the exhibition had once been the GHQ of General MacArthur and the Occupying forces, and now Gozo's works were finally being seen and enjoyed by the Japanese people.

As someone from Japan who has made the United States my home, I felt during the three years I spent researching Gozo Kawamura a continuous desire to express my gratitude to those Japanese people before me who pioneered life in the United States. I wanted to do my part to shine some light on the life of Gozo Kawamura, a Japanese man who is barely known in his home country.

I would especially like to express my gratitude to certain people. Much of my research centered at the City of Saku, Usuda Cultural Center. I am grateful to Masatoshi Maruyama, the former director, for helping me from the start to the finish of the project, gathering information and fact checking. I will never forget his kindness and warm character as he politely responded to each and every one of my persistent questions.

Also, I want to give special thanks to Masao Yoshikawa, of Maijisha Publishers, for encouraging me every time I was feeling like giving up on this project and for helping me to make it to the finish line. The writer and editor are two sides of a coin. If the communication between writer and editor is not going well, it can be very hard for them to work together. They have to work smoothly together with the same goal of producing a book. Many tens of phone calls, and many hundreds of faxes, passed between the United States and Japan. It took six long months. It was Masao Yoshikawa's perseverance that made the book possible. That we were able to see the book to completion makes me extremely happy.

I am deeply grateful to all the people who helped with the research materials and information necessary to publish this book.

December 1999
Nobuko Iinuma